MY Story

A FARM BOY FROM
A SMALL TOWN

JIM L. YOUNG

dustjacket

Dust Jacket Press
P.O. Box 721243
Oklahoma City, OK 73172
www.dustjacket.com

Cover and interior design: D. E. West / ZAQ Designs & Dust Jacket Creative Services

Printed in the United States of America

www.dustjacket.com

TABLE of CONTENTS

ACKNOWLEDGMENTS

I want to give a special thanks to my friend and Pastor, Mark Hollingsworth, for agreeing to edit this book for me. Without your help and encouragement, I would not have completed it. You are more than a Pastor to me, you're more like a brother from another mother and I love and appreciate you very much.

PREFACE

I decided to write this story after my 59th birthday, when I realized that my own children did not even know who I was or where I came from. They had always seen me in a wheelchair from the day they were born and probably never knew I had a rich full life as a kid growing up on a farm in northwest Oklahoma. They have never shown much interest in my family's history and if I should die they would not be able to share that history with their own children, so I decided to write this book not only for our four children but also for our ten grandchildren. I hope this book will not be too boring but will instead take my children and grandchildren on a journey back in time to see what life was like growing up in the 1960s and 1970s and the early years of the 1980s where we did not have many of the modern conveniences they have today. Furthermore, it is my hope that they will see all of the trials and tribulations I went through before and after my life changing accident and will appreciate how special and important each of them were to their mother and me, especially since we were not supposed to be able to have any children.

CHAPTER 1

My Family's Ancestry

I was born on June 4, 1960, the seventh and youngest child of Willis Edward Young and Evelyn Pauline (McDonald) Young. I have three older brothers and three older sisters. Barbara Louise (Braudrick) Maddox, and Billy Willis Braudrick are my oldest sister and brother who were born April 16, 1941 and October 21, 1942, respectively. For years we were led to believe that their father was George Braudrick, my mother's first husband who took his own life in 1945. It was not until my mother's last days that she confessed to me on her dying bed that Barbara and Billy were actually my full sister and brother and that daddy was actually their true father.

Mom and Dad were married on December 12, 1946 and a short time later my brother Charles Henry Young was born to this union on February 20, 1948 followed by my brother Larry Edward Young who was born on November 27, 1949. Belinda Ann (Young) Carter was born on March 24, 1955 and then Willneta Kay (Young) Mitchell was born on March 27,1959 and then myself, Jimmy Lee Young born June 4,1960, rounding out the seven children of Willis E. and Evelyn P. Young.

My father, Willis E. Young was the third oldest of eight children born to Charles Henry Young and Matilda Alma (Smith) Young on September 2, 1897, in Mountain Grove, Missouri. He died on our farm outside of Vici, Oklahoma on June 9, 1981 from a self-inflicted shotgun wound from my 12 gauge shotgun. His father Charles H. Young was born February 9, 1862, in Trumbull, Ohio, and died on March 18, 1956 at the age of 94 at Vici, Oklahoma. My grandfather and his older brother, William Edward Young, who was two years older than grandpa, were considered orphans during the Civil War and were actually raised by Dr. David L. Benson (a Union Doctor) and his wife Ester Benson in Perry County, Illinois, but later moved to Mountain Grove, Missouri in 1876. Their biological father was also known as William Edward Young and was born on December 29, 1829 in Addison, New York and died in Saline, Missouri on January 13,1886. He was a soldier in the Union army during the Civil War and was thought to have been killed in the war, but records show that he did not die until 1886, plus other records showed that he went on to father other children by two more women, other than Charles' and Williams' mother, Charlotte Bromley. Charlotte Bromley was born November 8, 1839 in Oswego, New York and died on October 20, 1884 at Mountain Grove, Missouri at the age of 44. Even though it has been told that Dr. Benson and his wife raised Charles and William after their father was believed to have been killed during the Civil War, I believe their mother Charlotte Bromley must have lived nearby since Dr. Benson and Charlotte Bromley both were buried at Mountain Grove, Missouri; Charlotte in 1884 and Dr. Benson in 1912.

My father's mother was Matilda Alma (Smith) Young and she was born on August 12, 1870 in Sullivan Indiana and died on May 6, 1959 at Vici, Oklahoma. She was 89 years of age and from all accounts of my aunts, uncles and cousins she was one of the best cooks around Vici, although my mother had to have been the second best. Both of my Young grandparents are buried at the South Persimmon Cemetery near Sharon, Oklahoma where my parents are also buried. I regret not getting to know my Young Grandparents as both died prior to me being born. I was told Grandpa was kind of mean and demanding while Grandma was kind and gentle and the best cook. Grandpa liked to raise fruit trees on the old sandy farm where they settled in 1916 and so I guess that passion passed on to me as

I have struggled for years to raise my own perfect fruit orchard which I am still striving to obtain.

Grandpa and Grandma Young were married December 21, 1890 and had eight children born to this union. The oldest was William Herbert Young born November 23, 1891, then Freddie Lawrence Young born, September 19, 1893, then my Father Willis Edward Young born, September 2, 1897, then Chelcie Lester Young born April 30, 1899, then Freeda Gladys (Young) Bowman born June 28, 1900, then Mabel Delphia (Young) Kruse born October 9, 1906, then Floyd Bryan Young born October 1, 1907 and finally Ester Charlotte (Young) Mc-Cray born July 24, 1911.

Sometime in 1916, Grandpa and Grandma Young sold their farm in Wright County, Missouri around Mountain Grove and moved to a farm north and west of Vici, Oklahoma. After researching the land deeds on the Young homestead which consisted of 240 acres in Section 25 and 80 acres in Section 30, it looks like Grandpa Young's brother William Edward Young originally bought the acreage on October 5, 1916 from Arthur and Eva Ray. We believe our Uncle Chelcie was the oldest of the children to make the move with my grandparents and the other younger children. Dad, when he was about 16 years of age, had already gone to Nebraska with his two older brothers, Herbert and Fred, to work on corn farms where they helped to cultivate and harvest corn. Herbert would later move to South

Dakota around Volga. Fred must have come back to Vici in 1919 because he purchased the 320 acre Young homestead from my Great Uncle W.E. and Great Aunt Annie May Young on May 12, 1919. He would only keep the place a short time in his name before selling or transferring the title to Grandpa and Grandma Young in 1923 and then he would go back to live in Missouri where he raised his family around Elk Creek, Missouri. Fred had served his country during World War I and fought in France and ironically was being transported back to the USA one week after the quit claim deed transferred the homestead to his name. The 1920 Census showed Grandpa and Grandma Young, Chelcie, Freeda, Mabel, Floyd and Ester living on the farm, but did not show Grandpa owning it but rather renting it in 1920. Dad would find his way back to Vici after Grandpa and Grandma Young had moved there, and Chelcie would go on to buy a farm just north of where my grandparents farm was located and he and my Aunt Fannie would raise their family. We called Chelcie Uncle Check and he was my favorite uncle, I guess because he just lived about five miles from our farm. My Aunt Freeda was my favorite aunt and she lived in Vici which was about 6 miles away from our farm. She helped take care of both Grandpa and Grandma Young in their old age. Next was my Aunt Mabel whom I grew to love and respect more, later in life, and who helped me get my life back on track with God. She and her husband Carl Kruse were evangelists with the Nazarene Church and they lived in Bethany, Oklahoma. Uncle Floyd looked like my dad even though he was ten years younger. He wore blue bibbed overalls while dad wore striped bib overalls and he had a full head of hair while my dad was bald. But if they were both wearing hats you could hardly tell them apart. My Aunt Ester lived in Idaho and we never got to see her and her family unless we had a family reunion or something. She was the youngest and turned out to outlive all of her siblings. She lived to be 92 years old. Only two of the siblings died in their 70's, Floyd at 72 and Chelcie at 74. The rest died in their 80's, except Aunt Ester. On the Young side of the family there were 38 grandchildren that ranged of being born in the year 1915 to 1960. I am the youngest of the 38 grandchildren or of the 1st cousins.

My Mother, Evelyn Pauline (McDonald) Young, went by the name of Lena. She was born in Springfield, Colorado, on May 19, 1915 while on harvest with her parents. She is the eldest of four children born to Irvin LeRoy (Roy) McDonald and Hazel Adeline (Bennett) McDonald. She died on April 24, 1992 from uterine cancer which had spread to all of her major organs. She was diagnosed with cancer on March 13, 1992 and lived about 6 weeks when she died in the Presbyterian Hospital in Oklahoma City. During her stay in the hospital, she always had one of her children or their spouses at her side. That's how special and important she was to us.

My mother's father was Irvin Leroy McDonald, who went by Roy. He was born July 29, 1892 in Smith County, Kansas and died on June 29, 1970 from injuries sustained from a pickup accident he had just 2 miles west of our farm. He had gone after some alfalfa hay at our neighbor's, George Altland, and was t-boned at the intersection by an oilfield worker. I had just turned 10 years old at the time. My grandfather McDonald's dad was John C. McDonald born July 17, 1862 in Racine, Wisconsin and died on August 3, 1917 at Woodward, Oklahoma from what they thought was stomach cancer. He was just 55 years old. My grandfather McDonald's mother was Evalena Agnes (McIlvain) McDonald who was born on September 15, 1867 in Wellman, Iowa and died in Vici, Oklahoma on November 14, 1908, shortly after giving birth to twins and from a rattlesnake bite. The girl twin also died while the boy twin lived. She went by the name of Eva and was only 41 years old when she died. John and Eva had six surviving children born to their union. The eldest was Ollie May (McDonald) Pfister born in 1890, then Irvin Leroy McDonald born in 1892 followed by Lynn Harold McDonald born in 1897, Ila Faye (McDonald) Mitchell born in 1904, Lile Clare (Bob) McDonald born in 1907, and Everett Floyd (Pete) McDonald born in 1908. Evalena Flo McDonald was the girl twin who did not survive birth in 1908. It is thought that John C. McDonald and Frank McCleery were the first two followers of the Church of the

First Born in Vici. John and Eva McDonald are buried at the Sunnyside Cemetery 6 miles east of Vici, Oklahoma.

My mother's mother was Hazel Adeline (Bennett) McDonald who was born August 30, 1894 in Nebraska. She died on August 16, 1984 at Vici, Oklahoma just 2 weeks short of her 90th birthday. She suffered from rheumatoid arthritis and type 1 diabetes, which left her confined to a wheelchair. She spent over thirteen years in a nursing home before dying. I hated nursing homes because of my grandmother having to stay in one.

Roy and Hazel McDonald were united in marriage on October 7, 1914 and five children were born to this union. My mother, Evelyn Pauline (Lena) was the eldest being born a short 7 months later on May 19, 1915. Five years later they had Estella Fern (McDonald) Killough, born on December 22, 1920 and died on July 7, 2003 at the age of 82. The next child, Jack Leroy McDonald did not survive and was born in 1924. Denver Dale McDonald was born on November 20, 1925 and died on January 11, 1975 when he committed suicide by stepping in front of a semi-truck. The youngest was Emery Keith McDonald born March 30, 1929 and died February 18, 2015 just short of his 86th birthday. In addition to their own children, my grandpa Roy and Grandma Hazel McDonald also took in two of grandpa's younger brothers to help raise after my Great Grandmother died in 1908 and Great Grandfather died in 1917. My mom was only 2 Years old when her grandfather died and her uncle Bob was only 10 and her uncle Pete was only 9, when they came to live with my grandparents. My grandfather McDonald's sister, Ollie, took the 13 year old sister Kaye to live with her.

From the McDonald side of my family there were only 14 grandchildren or 1st cousins from the four living children born to Roy and Hazel. Again, I was the youngest of the grandchildren and my siblings and I made up half of the total, or 7 out of the 14. Fern had two children, Betty Joanne and Everett Leroy Killough. Dale had 5 children Judy Dale, Diane Gale, Linda Sue, Arthur Roy and Gary Dale (Gimlit) McDonald. Keith never did have any children but his first wife Lois had a son, Butch, who had a daughter named Missy that Keith helped to raise.

Both of my Grandparents Roy and Hazel McDonald are buried at the Sunnyside Cemetery east of Vici, as well as their infant son Jack Leroy who shares a tombstone with them. Dale and Keith are also buried at the Sunnyside Cemetery.

C.H. Young Family
Back Row: Chelcie, Ester and Fred
Middle Row: Floyd, Mabel, Herbert, Freeda and Willis
Front Row: Charles H. Young and Matilda Alma Young

CHAPTER 2

Our Family and Farm

We lived on a 400 acre farm located 3 miles north and 3 miles west of Vici, Oklahoma. The acreage was split up into two 80 acres tracts of land that ran parallel to one another, separated by the county road that ran in front of our house. Then there was the Antis Place which connected to the south 80 acres which consisted of 160 acres of wheat and pasture. My dad had bought this land in 1926 with his father and it was here that he had share cropped with George and Evelyn Braudrick, my mother. Then we had an additional 80 acres of pasture land about 1-1/2 miles west of our house and ½ mile south that my dad had bought across from the original Young homestead, where my Grandpa and Grandma Young had lived before moving to town. The north 80 acres is where our house and barn were located. The farm house was a white stucco house with 3 bedrooms, 1 bath, living room, dining room, kitchen, utility room, basement and a separator room for separating the cream from the milk. It wasn't a huge house but it wasn't small either. By the time I came along, it had already served the purpose of a home for my older sister and brother who had already moved out and were starting their own families. The house originally had 4 bedrooms and no bathroom until my Uncle Floyd help convert two of the bedrooms into one bedroom with closets, a hallway, and a bathroom with a tub. Charles contends the conversion happened in 1957 while Barbara says it happened after she was married in 1958 or 1959.

Barbara had already married her high school sweetheart Joe Maddox on August 24, 1958 and by the time I was born, I was an uncle to my niece Sandy Maddox born May 14, 1959. A little over year after I was born, Gayla Maddox came along on August 29, 1961 and then Jody Maddox four years later on July 23, 1964. Because of our closeness in age, my nieces and nephew seemed more like 1st cousins to me and we were best of friends and could not wait to see one another. Barbara and her family lived in Woodward about 20 miles away from our farm but it seemed like an all-day drive when riding with mom or dad to go see them. Joe and Barbara have been married for over 60 years and live in the same house on Main Street that they built in the 1960s. Joe worked at Starr Lumber in Woodward for years before starting his own business blowing insulation and later installing garage doors. During this time he also worked as a voluntary firefighter and later as a full time firefighter while running his businesses. He retired from the Woodward Fire Dept. after 30 years. Barbara did babysitting, cleaned houses and helped Joe with the books for his businesses, but Joe pretty much provided for their family. Barbara had ovarian cancer in her forties and is considered a cancer survivor for the past thirty plus years.

Billy graduated in 1960, the year I was born, so I don't ever remember him living at our farm house. He told me that after graduating from high school he lived at the farm for a while, with Barbara and Joe for a while or where ever he could find to live. He was figuring out life, working odd jobs, going on harvest with my Uncle Keith, working on ranches or at the lumberyard with my brother-in-law Joe and then he married Wanna Maddox, Joe's sister, on April 19, 1963. They lived in Liberal, Kansas from February 1964 to January 1968, where Billy worked for Beech Aircraft. On June 16, 1964 Joe Mac Braudrick was born followed by Teresa Braudrick born on September 24, 1966. I now had three nieces and 2 nephews to play with. Billy and Wanna moved back to Woodward in 1968 where Billy worked for Mistletoe Express part of the day and the DX gas station part of the day. They then moved to Fargo,

Oklahoma and worked for Sutter Ranch until March 1970 when they moved back to Vici and lived at Howard Borden's old farm and worked for Harold Hutchison's ranch. We were so excited that Joe Mac and Teresa only lived a few miles from us. In 1971 they were given the opportunity to manage Broce Pony Ranch in Evergreen, Colorado for Ray Broce, who owned Broce Construction Company. They moved their family to Evergreen in 1971 and managed the ranch for nine years before moving back to Vici, Oklahoma in 1980. Billy then worked in heavy construction for McNeil Construction operating a road grader, building well sites and lease roads or working on highway construction. They later moved to Woodward after both of their kids would have completed high school, where Wanna worked for Chase Appliance and Billy for Diamond Construction. He retired in about 2015 and they moved back to Vici and now live in the house next to where our Grandpa and Grandma Young lived when they retired. Billy and Barbara have always been close being the oldest of the siblings but Billy, Larry and I have become closer by reminiscing about the past. Billy and Larry have been instrumental in helping me recall some of the events written in this book.

Charles and Larry were still in high school at my earliest recollection. They shared the north bedroom of our house while Belinda and Willneta shared the middle bedroom and mom and dad shared the south bedroom. I slept on the sofa back then as far as I can remember, later I would move into the north bedroom when Charles moved out and went to college and prior to enlisting in the Navy.

Charles graduated in 1966, the year I started to school. He went to college at Panhandle A&M in Goodwell, Oklahoma in the fall of 1966 and spring of 1967. After he started to college he purchased a motorcycle from Wendell Jones who owned an automotive repair shop in Vici, who also sold motorcycles. When daddy found out, he made Charles take the motorcycle back and get his money refunded.

In July of 1967 Charles found out from the draft board that his status had changed from a 1S (Student) to a 1A (available) and that he would most likely be drafted to go to Vietnam in the Marines or the Army within the next month. Charles instead decided to enlist in the Navy and the recruiting officer assured him that he could get him into Aviation Electronics training after boot camp on a deferred enlistment program, where he would not have to report until November of 1967. Furthermore, he promised him that his one year of college would allow him to come out of boot camp as an E-3 pay grade.

Shortly after Charles had signed up for the Navy he met a girl who had come back to Vici with her foster parents, John and Donna West from Michigan to visit their relatives who lived in Vici. Her name was Nina Zeidell, and Charles fell head over heels in love with her, and in fact, when they went back to Michigan, Charles did too, driving a blue 1963 GMC V-6 Pickup he had purchased. He had told mom that he was going to Michigan but never let daddy know anything about it, probably because he figured daddy wouldn't let him go. He found employment at Consolidated Container Corp. which made cardboard boxes. He quickly learned how to make boxes and was in no time mastering how to set up the machines to make the bends in the boxes and place labels on them. He worked there until he and Nina came back to Vici in October of 1967. When they came back they were already married and lived with us about a month before Charles had to report for basic training in San Diego, California. Charles found employment that month helping a neighbor who lived about 8 or 9 miles east of us cut down large cottonwood trees around Gage, Oklahoma. His name was Roy Remmele, and after Charles went to basic training, he was killed by the tree limb of one of the large cottonwood trees he had cut down. This happened on November 16, 1967 and he was probably the first person I remember dying and having a funeral.

The month that Charles and Nina lived with us was always filled with drama. My sister Belinda didn't get along with Nina and my dad did not care for Nina smoking around us kids. And then there was the constant fighting and yelling between Charles and Nina. I had told myself that I was never going to get married if this is what marriage was all about. I remember one time I was going to our bathroom and looked down the hall into the bedroom where Charles and Nina slept and there was Nina standing there buck naked. I think this was the first time I had seen an adult woman in the nude. I was a little over seven years old at the time.

When Charles finally went to basic training in San Diego, California they had to figure out where Nina was going to stay for the next 12 weeks. At first, she stayed at our house and my mom tried to show her how to sew. Nina had a temper and would get frustrated and start yelling at my mom. One day she got so frustrated and mad that she stormed out of the house and started walking over to my Grandpa and Grandma Mc-Donalds, and that's where she ended up living. After all Grandpa McDonald smoked cigarettes that he rolled himself using Prince Albert tobacco in a can and he would not mind Nina smoking. Belinda was even more displeased by Nina staying with Grandpa McDonald because she was very jealous having to share her Grandpa with Nina.

Charles completed his basic training at San Diego and came back to Vici to get his new wife, who was now pregnant and moved her and their belongings to Jacksonville, Florida where he was to go through his Aviation Electronics training. He said that our Uncle Albert Bowman helped him build side boards for his 1963 GMC pickup and then drape a tarp across the top to keep his belongings out of the rain while they drove across the country to Jacksonville. He completed his aviation electronics training and on July 23, 1968 they had their first child, Charles Henry Young, Jr., but we called him Chucky. About two years later on February 20, 1970, which was also Charles' birthdate, they had their second child Tammy Young. Unfortunately, Charles and Nina were not able to make their marriage work and they divorced sometime in 1972.

Charles would go on to serve ten years in the Navy, re-enlisting after his initial 4 year enlistment and serving another 6 years, getting out of the Navy in 1977. While in the Navy he served on the aircraft carrier USS Forrestal, the same aircraft carrier that John McCain had served on and had started a bad fire on the flight deck that took months to repair. The last carrier he served on was the USS Nimitz, one of the first nuclear powered class carrier. He reached the pay grade of an E-6 and the title of Aviation Fire Control Tech First Class. His job was to maintain the fire control radar and computers that locked in on targets and fired missiles from the F-14 fighter jets.

He would go on to remarry a southern girl from Mobile, AL named Connie Stein on February 24, 1973, that he had met while stationed in Memphis, TN and they would have a son, Nathan Young, who was born April 15, 1982. Charles and Connie moved back to Vici to help dad farm in 1977. Me and a friend, Kenny Campbell, flew out there to help them load up and move back to Vici. They stayed and helped on the farm while I went off to college but later moved to Colorado outside of Victor where Charles pursued his construction skills and then they moved back to Connie's home town of Mobile, AL where they too were divorced in 2002 after almost 30 years of marriage. He would later meet another Alabama girl, Patricia that he married in 2005 and is currently married to.

Charles has made his career after the Navy doing construction and remodel work, forming a company called Golden Hammer Construction. He has always been the most talented of all of us kids and can do about anything he puts his mind to. His 2nd wife Connie used to say that she wished he wasn't so smart because she would like to get something new every once in a while. Instead, if a hair dryer would break, he would open it up, figure out what was broken and repair it.

I remember Charles always reloading shotgun shells out in the building next to our house where we kept our cream cans in a refrigerator. It was kind of his shop and work area. He also reloaded shotgun shells with rock salt to keep watermelon thieves out of our watermelon patch south of the house. Teenagers from town knew dad grew big black diamond watermelons, so there were constant attempts made on our watermelons by the teenagers. Charles and Larry were on call to run them off and I heard that they sometimes put sugar in their gas tanks while the thieves were in the watermelon patch.

There were many stories that I heard over the years about Charles and Larry. One was about them when they were about 6 and 4, and Charles decided to dig a hole in the sand out by the pig pen. He dug a deep hole, then got in it and started pulling the sand back in around his body until all of the sudden he couldn't get out of the hole. He had to have Larry go get daddy to dig him out. I think daddy made him dig himself out to teach him a lesson. Then one time Charles and Larry saw a bright orange thing on the north edge of our alfalfa field, east of our house. It was weather balloon and had a box attached to it that had a Georgia address of where to send the box should someone find it. They just knew that they would receive some type of reward if they mailed the box back. They sent off the box and waited patiently for the reward money to come rolling in but instead just got a letter thanking them for returning it. I guess there was a parachute attached to the box that they thought they would be able to use if they got up high enough on something, so Charles attached the parachute to his body and climbed to the top of a large hay stack and jumped off. A big wind came up and swept the parachute and Charles across the north pasture over plumb thickets and into our neighbor's barbed wire fence. Charles was all cut and scratched up and never tried that again. The parachute was retired after one use.

Larry graduated in May 1968, my second grade year. He was a little over 10 years older than me and I looked up to him as my hero and role model as a young boy. My father was 62 years 9 months old when I was born so he never took me fishing or hunting or anything fun, or so I thought. Larry used to let me ride in his first car, a white 1960 Chevrolet Bel-Air with the big back fins. He called it the "White Lizard" and we used to take it across the south pasture to go retrieve the milk cows for their evening milking. We would listen to AM 1520 KOMA out of Oklahoma City on the radio to CCR (Credence Clearwater Revival) or other bands that sang about the Vietnam War that was heating up over in Southeast Asia, most of which were songs protesting the war. It was turbulent and divided times in the United States as college students and young adult men and women were expressing their rights of freedom of speech and staging protests to the war. Hippies were popping up everywhere and the use of illegal drugs was becoming more and more prevalent. Marijuana use was widespread that lead to more dangerous drugs like LSD, acid and heroine. I remember my dad worrying about losing control of his own boys and them becoming hippies like we were seeing on TV. I tried to make sure my hair was cut short not to disappoint my dad.

Larry graduated from high school and went to Northwestern State University in Alva, Oklahoma the fall of 1968, the spring of 1969 and the fall of 1969 when he was contacted by an Army recruiter in January 1970 that his number was coming up and that he would either be drafted in the Army in February or March of 1970. He asked Larry to come up and visit him at the recruiting office where he presented Larry with a deal he couldn't refuse. He told Larry if he signed up for the Army that he would get him into NCO (Non Commissioned Officer) school and that he would make the rank of an E-5 Sergeant after graduating. I guess he was pretty persuasive and Larry signed up for a 2 week deferred enlistment program in the U.S. Army. By February 20, 1970 which was our niece Tammy Young's birthdate, Larry was in Oklahoma City spending the night at the Black Hotel where enlistees were being processed and sent on busses to Fort Leonard Wood, Missouri for basic training. He spent 8 weeks in basic training, 8 weeks in AIT (Advance Individual Training) school and then onto NCO engineer school where he graduated 3rd in his class. When he graduated he was told that he and the first two in his class would have ordinarily been given the rank of an E-6 meaning three stripes on top with one rocker below, but because the Army had so many NCOs they were only given a rank of E-5,three stripes on top, or a Sergeant. They were told, should an opening occur, they would be the first three considered for a promotion to the rank of Staff Sergeant or an E-6. Because Larry had enlisted instead of being drafted, he was supposed to be able to choose the area that he was to be trained in and he chose the engineers. So happened that there were two Larry E. Young's in his platoon and squad, and he got the draftees orders while the other Larry E. Young got his orders and which would have sent Larry to California for combat infantry rather than staying at Ft. Leonard Wood for engineer training. Larry told his commander that there had been a mix up and what had happened and they got it corrected. It was my Cousin Benny Young that got Larry to be transferred into the 101st Airborne Division in Vietnam.

Larry shipped out for his one year tour of duty in Vietnam in January 1971 from OKC to LAX where they took a bus to Oakland, California to await their muster orders to be flown to Anchorage, AK and then on to Yokohama Japan. From there they flew into Bien Hoa, Vietnam onboard a commercial TWA flight. From there they were bussed to Long Bien. Their first night in Long Bien they took in a live band concert put on by the USO and they were mortared during the show. The next day they took a C-130 transport plane from Bien Hoa to Phu Bai and this is where they checked in their class "A" uniforms and received their jungle clothing, boots, weapons and other gear. Their first night at Phu Bai they were again mortared. From there they made their way to Camp Evans traveling in 5 ton trucks that were lined with sand bags in the floor in case of running over mines to avoid casualties. Camp Evans was where my first cousin Benny Young was stationed with the 101st Airborne Division. Larry was in SERTs (Screaming Eagle Recruit Training School) training at Camp Evans when he heard a familiar voice outside the barracks say "Hey you don't have a Larry Young in there, do you?" It was Benny who was a Sergeant First Class E-7. Benny told Larry to leave his duffle bag at Camp Evans and they took Larry's first helicopter ride down to Camp Eagle where Larry was supposed to report. Camp Eagle was located between Hue and Phu Bai. Benny thought that he could get Larry assigned to Camp Evans with him, but when they got to Camp Eagle they were told that the Army would not let two NCOs that were related, to be assigned to the same company. Larry explained that his duffle bag was still at Camp Evans and they said well you better go get it and report back here. At that time there was an Assistant PSNCO (Personnel Staff NCO) E-5 Sergeant Gripka that was a short timer waiting to be shipped back to the states. They asked Larry if he knew how to type. To which he answered yes and his orders were changed from combat engineers to Personnel Staff and he was assigned to Personnel S1 as the company's assistant PSNCO. He processed new personnel coming into Camp Eagle and acclimated them to their area of operations.

Larry's derose date started on 13-Jan-1971 and his tour of duty should have lasted until 12-Jan-1972, but because they were drawing back the number of the troops, he actually got to ship out on 20-Dec-1971, 21 days early. Coming back to the states he went from Camp Eagle to Da Nang Airport where they flew him back to Ft Lewis, just outside of Seattle, WA.

They fed them a steak and potato meal at Ft. Lewis, took back their jungle fatigues and boots and reissued them their class "A" dress uniforms and gave them their orders to where they were to go. Larry's orders said to Vici, Oklahoma. So he and some other buddies caught a taxi to go to the Seattle airport to catch a flight to Dallas Texas. He said the taxi driver was driving like 55 to 60 MPH on the slick roads being covered by snow and he just knew they were going to crash. He had been used to riding in vehicles going like 15 to 20 MPH back in Vietnam so this was the first thing that struck him different upon returning to the United States. The second thing that struck him different was when he got to the Dallas Airport people were talking so that he could understand everything they were saying. He had been used to hearing people talk in Vietnamese and Chinese and now all of the sudden everyone was speaking the same language, English. From Dallas he flew into Will Rogers Airport in OKC and then took a taxi to the Union Bus Terminal in Oklahoma City to catch a bus to Woodward, Oklahoma. He arrived at Woodward at 10:30 pm that night and called Barbara and Joe who took him back to their house. He would call mom the next morning and then he came down to the farm and mom was kissing him and crying in relief that he had made it home unharmed.

Larry got to spend Christmas with us in 1971 instead of Vietnam because he got to return 21 days earlier than originally scheduled. It was a great Christmas and I got a five year diary amongst other items for Christmas. I back dated a couple of journal entries to include Dec. 21, 1971 where Larry came home, but also to write down that Larry, James and Kenny Randall and our 2nd cousin Mickey Young had had a car wreck Christmas eve. Larry ran off the highway where it curves and hit an embankment of sand. It had been foggy that night and he misjudged the curve. Larry sustained a cut nose but the other boys were not injured.

While Larry was still on leave a blizzard happened on January 3, 1972. My Uncle Joe Killough was killed when his car stalled on the railroad tracks in Liberal, Kansas on his way to work. The impact of the train broke his neck. This was my mom's sister Fern's husband. On January 5, 1972 I was going to the barn to help milk cows when Snoopy barked at a car parked under the mulberry trees, it was Charles, Nina, Chucky and Tammy. They called for me to come over because they thought I had already seen them and wanted me to keep quiet so they could surprise everyone. We had Uncle Joe's funeral in Liberal, Kansas on January 8, 1972. Since Larry and Charles were both home, on January 12, 1972 we had a surprise 25th wedding anniversary for Mom and Dad. Their actual anniversary had been on Dec 12, 1971.

Charles, Nina and their kids stayed with us until January 17, 1972. Larry had to report to Ft. Carson in Colorado

Springs, Colorado so him and mom went first to Billy and Wanna's place in Evergreen, Colorado on January 22, 1972. They left at about 5:00 am and never woke me so I never got to say good bye to Larry. Mom called us from Billy's house that evening after they arrived. Wanna and their kids would later bring mom back home and Larry reported for his final year in the Army at Ft. Carson.

Larry spent his final year at Ft. Carson and was released on March 19, 1973, because he had to extend for one month while taking Police Science training at the El Paso Community College to be in law enforcement. After his hitch was up in the Army he hired on to Jefferson County, Colorado as a deputy sheriff. It was there that he met his first wife Tonya and they were married shortly thereafter in July 1973. He worked in Jefferson County about a year before he and Tonya moved back to Vici, Oklahoma and Larry worked for my brother-in-law Joe Maddox blowing insulation into homes. On June 16, 1974 after coming home one evening Larry and Tonya had a fight and Tonya took Larry's service revolver and shot herself. They were living at my Grandpa and Grandma McDonald's old rock house at the time. Tonya is buried at South Persimmon Cemetery near Sharon, Oklahoma where my parents are buried. She was 34 years old at the time of her passing. Larry was ten years younger than Tonya.

After Tonya's death Larry moved to Woodward and started

his career in the oil patch. He has worked for many drilling companies over the past 41 years, working his way up from a floor hand, derrick hand, driller, tool pusher to drilling superintendent and company man. While working in the oilfield, he married his second wife Helen Gipson on March 9, 1977 and they had two daughters born, Tina Lorene Young on January 24, 1978 and Priscilla Lynn Young on November 14, 1984. They lost one son at birth whom they had named Tyson on November 4, 1979. Larry and Helen were divorced in 2003 and Larry would later marry Retha McBroom whom he is married to today. They never had any children together but are raising Retha's granddaughter Ciera.

Belinda was five years older than me and graduated in 1973. Of course she, Willneta and I were the youngest of the seven children so we were probably the closest to one another and still are today. Belinda has worked in finance or accounting ever since she graduated from High School, in fact I think she was probably working at the Bank of Vici while still in high school. After she left the Bank of Vici and graduated from school she moved to Woodward, Oklahoma and lived in a small 1 bedroom house behind Mrs. Johnson's son and daughter-in-law, Leland and Evelyn Johnson at Woodward, Oklahoma. She found employment at Woodward working for Melvin Johnston & Stan Hawthorne, CPAs in May 1973 and worked there for 2 ½ years and then went to work for 2M Drilling for 2 years, before they sold out. In March of 1978 she went to work for Buster Forbes, a mud engineer doing his invoicing, payroll reports and bookkeeping. In March of 1981 she went to work for Stephanie Craighead, CPA until February of 1988. After that she worked for Jeter Well Service from February 1988 to July 1989 and then American Logging from July 1989 to July 1996. After that she worked at Hooper Construction from July 1996 to May of 2000. She was off 5 months of 2000 but found part-time work doing books for David Cramer who had several companies. She continued doing part-time work for David even after she found full time work at Northwest Center for Behavior Health, a state government agency from June 3, 2002 until her retirement on May 31, 2019.

Belinda married Bill Carter on June 11, 1976 and two boys were born to this union, Mark Allen Carter on May 20, 1977 followed by Michael Edward Carter on October 5, 1979. They originally lived in the small one bedroom house that Belinda lived in Woodward, but the ceilings in that house were only about six feet tall and Bill stood about 6'4". They then purchased a mobile home and moved to Southdown's Trailer Park on the south side of Woodward, before finally moving to Fargo in about 1984. Both Mark and Michael would graduate from the Fargo High School in 1996 and 1998, respectively. Sadly, we lost Michael shortly after his 30th birthday on December 13, 2009 after battling Crohn's disease and ultimately brain cancer caused by the drugs used to fight Crohn's. Bill was a truck driver and worked in construction eventually working for himself until his health declined and he had to be placed in a nursing home in Weatherford, Oklahoma and later in the Vici Nursing Home Center in Vici, Oklahoma. Bill passed away on April 4, 2018.

Willneta married the love of her life on my birthday June 4, 1977, his name was Kerry Mitchell and he was from Yale, Oklahoma. Kerry and his dad and some of his brothers worked for Skinner Construction Company out of Yale and they were building oil tanks for a refinery out west of town near Harmon, Oklahoma. Willneta worked at D&K Cafe as a waitress and this is where they met and fell in love. Willneta traveled with Kerry living in a 20' travel trailer they pulled behind their pickup all over the country building oil tanks, even as far as North Carolina. Meanwhile, two children were born to this union, Jeremy Bryce Mitchell on March 16, 1980 and Kera Dawn Mitchell on April 8, 1981. Willneta and Kerry moved back to Oklahoma in December 1982 and Kerry went to work for Tonkawa Refinery where he had built oil tanks back in 1977 near Harmon, Oklahoma. They moved their travel trailer to Fargo, Oklahoma and Willneta went to work for Melvin Johnston, CPA where I had started working in August 1982. Kerry then found work at the Department of Transportation Division 6 office in Buffalo, Oklahoma in July 1984, where

Kathy's mom and dad worked. Dean, Kathy's had, helped him get the job. Kerry has worked his way up the ladder to becoming Transportation Superintendent II for Division 6 for the State of Oklahoma. They rented our Lancer Mobile home for several years after we moved from Fargo until they bought their own home in Fargo and then in November 2005 they sold their home and moved to Buffalo when the state would no longer allow Kerry to drive a state vehicle from Woodward to Buffalo. Willneta continued to work for Melvin Johnston as an accountant until the April 2006 tax season was over. She then went to work for Pioneer Abstract in Buffalo while still cleaning Melvin's office in Fargo. Later in 2012 she took a position with Harper County as a Deputy County Clerk, which she is currently working today. She is still cleaning Melvin Johnston's old CPA office which was sold to Becky Ladd, CPA several years ago after Melvin retired. All three of us youngest children Belinda, Willneta and I worked for Melvin Johnston, but Willneta worked for him almost 23 years.

Willneta and Kerry have been very involved in the Fargo Church of the Nazarene, serving on the board, leading the songs on Sunday mornings or teaching Sunday School Classes. Willneta also contributes her time visiting the elderly in nursing homes at Buffalo, Woodward and Vici.

Willi E. Young Family taken in July 1970
Back Row: Billy, Barbara, Larry, Belinda and Charles
Front Row: Willneta, Willis, Lena and Jimmy

Older Siblings: Back row: Barbara & Billy
Front Row: Larry and Charles

Younger siblings: Belinda, Willneta and Jimmy

Our 3 bedroom stucco house

CHAPTER 3

More About My Parents

To really understand the dynamics of my childhood, you had to know more about my parents. You had to realize that my parents were the age of most of my classmate's grandparent's and even some of their great-grandparents. Both had lived through the Great Depression of the 1930's and World War II, and for my dad even World War I, so they both knew what it was like to sacrifice, ration and be conservative with what they had. This was a value that they passed on to us children. We did not waste food and appreciated what we had to eat at the dinner table. We may have not liked certain food but we always cleaned our plates and if we had leftovers that was the next day's dinner or supper. Yes, back then we called our meals breakfast, dinner and supper.

My Dad was almost 63 years old when I was born, so I never saw him as the young daring man that he had been in his earlier years. He graduated the 8th grade from the Broyles School, in Hartville, Missouri. in 1912 and then he left with his two older brothers Herbert and Fred to find employment working in Nebraska planting, cultivating, and harvesting corn. We believe he worked in Nebraska from 1913 – 1917 before catching up with his parents and younger siblings that had moved to Northwest Oklahoma in 1916.

From 1917 - 1922 he worked at the Midco Gasoline Company at Billings, Oklahoma a gasoline refinery. While working there he was burned during a fire and spent several weeks in St. Mary Hospital in Enid, Oklahoma healing. He registered for the draft in 1919 during World War I but was not selected for service.

He probably came back to Vici and helped Grandpa Young farm after he worked at the refinery in Billings at least until he headed to Oregon and Washington State to become a lumberjack. One of his little black books showed that he was cutting timber as early as May 1923 through 1924. None of his black books showed him cutting timber in 1925. After researching the ownership of the Young Homestead, it became apparent that my dad and Grandpa went into a partnership with one another running the Old Ray place that Grandpa took title to on June 20, 1923 from my Uncle Fred. On August 27, 1925, Grandpa and Grandma Young transferred one half interest in the 320 acre Young Homestead to daddy. Daddy then went back to around Bend and Kirk, Oregon from February 1926 to May 1926 and cut more timber. That year he and his partner harvested over 1,063 trees and some 1,422,900 board feet of lumber. He then came back to Vici in 1926 and he and Grandpa Young purchased the Antis place on August 2, 1926, a 160 acre tract of land that he farmed until his death in 1981. He returned back to Oregon in 1928 where he and his partner, possibly Carl Seaburn, harvested another 2,629 trees or 3,520,530 board feet of lumber from two different lumber camps, Ervansca and Pelican Bay. Then from January to May 1929 he and his partner harvested another 1,850 trees or 3,445,110 board feet of lumber at the Big Lake Box Co. and Pelican Bay lumber camps. He had documented all of his lumberjacking days in two little black log books that he maintained.

It was the Antis place that daddy share cropped with George and Evelyn Braudrick during the late 1930's and early 1940's. The 1930 census shows daddy living with Grandpa and Grandma Young along with my first cousin Burl Young, Herbert's son born in 1917. The 1940 census showed daddy living in the same house as George and Evelyn Braudrick, his hired hand and wife.

In 1942, daddy would go to Alaska along with two other Vici men, Loyd Helmick and Bob Mercer for the Civil Engineers, Department of the Army helping to build airstrips and highways during World War II. Daddy kept a five year diary while in Alaska that I think started in April 1942 and ended in May 1945. He worked as an oiler on heavy equipment, working his way up to a Heavy Equipment Mechanic making $1.75 per hour to eventually a General Manager over a group of men. His work would stretch from Fairbanks, Alaska to the Aleutian Islands. Story goes that he won a big jackpot gambling on what day the ice would melt where they were working. Several men had picked the same day as he had so they split the jackpot and he still got like $8,000 for his share. This is how he afforded to buy our home place from Carl Mote later in 1947.

Before daddy came back from Alaska in May 1945, George Braudrick committed suicide on February 1, 1945, leaving mom a widow with two small children to raise. Daddy came home in May 1945 and he and mom were married on December 12, 1946. Prior to daddy coming back from Alaska, mom, Barbara and Billy lived with Grandpa and Grandma McDonald.

We believe daddy and Grandpa McDonald went on harvest the summer of 1946, going all the way up to North Dakota. Back then the combine they used was pulled by a tractor belonging to dad, a 1936 Farmall F-20, which only produced

28 HP. The combine was either an old Massey Harris or an old M&M. Based on a little black book that daddy kept records of their expenses, I would say the combine was a M&M because several parts purchased said M&M parts. The combine had its own engine that ran the belts and chains, the pulleys and idler pulleys that turned the reel operating the cutter cycle bar and the thrasher that separated the grain from the wheat head. Not sure what kind of truck Grandpa had back then.

Daddy delivered papers for High Plains Journal or Farmer's Stockman during 1946 and 1947, and then he bought Carl Mote's place on December 20, 1947 and moved Mom and my two older siblings to our home place. Previous to moving to the farm, they had lived in a small house in town. With the purchase of the Mote place, he now had a 4 bedroom house with no bathroom and a huge barn to pursue milking cows, raising wheat, raising and cutting hay and running cattle on pasture. I was even told by Billy and Larry that daddy raised sheep during the early years. No sheep were ever seen on the farm during my childhood. On December 29, 1951 daddy and Grandpa settled up on their partnership and Grandpa deeded his half of the Antis place back to daddy and half of the west 80 from the original homestead back to daddy. In return daddy deeded back his half of the original 240 acres of the homestead back to Grandpa and Grandma Young. This 240 acres would then be sold to G.T Redwine on December 5, 1955 prior to

Grandpa dying in March of 1956. Daddy's farm was now complete with the 400 acres, I described earlier, until he sold off the west 80 acres to Merle Guthrie in 1975, to help pay for mom's hip surgery.

I don't hardly remember a time when my dad was not working on the farm, either milking cows, hoeing the garden, hoeing the watermelon patch or corn patch, hauling hay, unloading feed, working cattle and hogs, building fence, cutting fence posts, baling hay, plowing fields or planting wheat. He could spend all day out in the hot sun and only come in at noon to eat dinner with mom, watch "As the World Turns" on TV then go back out in the heat and plow until it was time to milk the cows. He never had a good water jug to take with him out to the fields until my brother Charles and his 2nd wife, Connie bought him a Coleman Thermos jug to put ice and water in. He thought that little red and white jug was quite the thing. Before the Coleman thermos, he used an old glass gallon jar with a lid, he wrapped a burlap sack around to keep the water cool. He would sit it behind a fence post or in some weeds to shade it from the sun and then would visit it during the day when he got thirsty.

We always had Border collie dogs that dad had control of. He could command them to go get the cattle out in the north 80. If the dog did not bring all of the cows or calves into the corral daddy would say, "that's not all of them" and the dog would turn around and go get the rest of them. One of those dogs that he had at the end would just follow him around all day out in the field while he was plowing. The dog before that was named Snoopy. We had him for 13 years before coyotes tore him up and he died in 1980. He saved daddy on February 25, 1972 after a bull rolled daddy while he was leading the bull to the stock tank. The bull rebelled because a cow was in heat and the bull had other things on his mind than being led by a nose ring. He got dad down and started rolling him. Snoopy was right there and on that bull's ankles immediately and saved dad. The doctor said daddy had pleurisy from being rolled. My Uncle Floyd and Larry Brown, a neighbor boy helped me do chores for several weeks while daddy recovered.

I remember helping my dad build fence on the Antis place when I was 18 years old and he was 81. I had been out drinking the night before and he knew it, so he had me working off the alcohol in the hot sun. Even at 81 he could still outwork most teenagers. He was just that kind of man. He suffered from depression especially in the last years but he would not give up and leave the farm. He did not want to spend his last days in a nursing home, so he took what he thought was the only way out. I just wished I could have been there to talk him out of it.

My mom was 45 when I was born, almost 18 years younger than my dad. She was the oldest of her siblings, had survived the Great Depression, World War II and the suicide of her first husband. She had a heart bigger than Texas, and dearly loved each and every one of her 7 children. She had inherited the trait of being a "worry wort" from her father and she had become a wonderful cook, which may have been passed down from her mother, but I really don't remember Grandma McDonald cooking that much because she was confined to a wheelchair when I was about 8 or 9 years old. I remember her making dill pickles from cucumbers and dill that Grandpa McDonald grew in his dark rich soil of his garden, but I really don't remember her cooking much.

I don't ever remember eating anything that mom cooked that wasn't good. She had the flair for making something out of nothing and could conjure up about any kind of desert, jam, jelly or preserve you could think of. My favorite jam I guess you would call it was apricot butter. We had about 3 large apricot trees in our tree rows south of the house that would produce apricots about once every 5 to 8 years, if a late frost did not get them. Half the time when they did produce, the fruit would be wormy but this never stopped mom from turning this fruit into the most wonderful apricot butter to eat on your pancakes or biscuits. My second favorite jelly was black currant jelly, made from the currants that grew wild along both sides of the road in front of our house. I knew that if I wanted any currant jelly I would have to go pick currants, so Belinda, Willneta and I would always go pick them knowing what was to come. Then we had a blackberry patch out east of our house on the north side of our large garden, where we raised potatoes and corn. The blackberry plants were of the thorn type and boy would they tear up your arms and hands when you went to pick them, not to mention the wasps, chiggers and mosquitoes that would eat you up. But, the by product was either fresh blackberries over a white pound cake that mom baked, blackberry cobbler, blackberry jelly or blackberry ice cream made from the fresh cream she separated from the cows we milked. There was always red sand plum jelly made from wild sand plum thickets on our place or maybe wild grape jelly made from wild grapes that grew alongside the road over by our west 80. And then there were the yellow pear tomato preserves and watermelon preserves and persimmon pudding made from persimmon trees that grew east of our Grandpa McDonald's place or on our Uncle Buck and Aunt Francis Hutchen's place. If there was a fruit available mom would turn it into something delicious to eat.

Mom's homemade bread rolls were second to none and with the same recipe she could make mouth-watering cinnamon rolls that would melt in your mouth. She made everything fresh using cream she separated or butter that she churned. We always had a gallon jar of whole milk in the refrigerator with a layer of cream on the top that you have to blow back to pour the milk. The rest of the milk we got from milking cows was run through our McCormick cream separator back in the utility room. We milked 7 to 14 cows in the mornings and evenings seven days a week. The separator had two out spouts, one for milk and one for cream. The cream would be collected in 5 or 10 gallon cream cans and placed in an old refrigerator in the black building next to our house. Once a week a truck from Gold Spot Creamery out of Enid would come by and collect the full cream cans and leave us two empty cream cans to fill. One of the drivers for Gold Spot was Hop Salisbury, the father of one of my friends, Danny. The cream cans normally had your designated number painted on the lids or cans itself to identify which cans belonged to which farmer. Our number was 7483. The separated milk, or slop as we called it, was caught in 5 gallon buckets and taken out to the hogs to eat or maybe mixed in chicken feed to give the chickens a little extra moisture in their feed. I remember mom or dad mixing up that chicken feed with milk and sitting it on the floor furnace in our dining room to warm it up before feeding it to the chickens. Man, I can still smell the odor that came off that concoction. It smelled awful!

My mom's homemade ice cream could not be beat. She made vanilla, chocolate, strawberry, blackberry or pineapple ice cream using the cream we separated and the milk we collected and the eggs we gathered. In addition, to the ice cream she made a chocolate cake with a runny chocolate frosting that was to die for and then to top it off she would make a pitcher of that same runny frosting to put on top of your ice cream. It was nothing for uncles and aunts, cousins and neighbors to come to our house and eat ice cream and cake with us.

Sundays were always special days to us. We would attend church, swing by James Andrews Phillips 66 station and have him grind up a big chunk of ice and put it in a thick paper bag for making ice cream, then go pick up my grandma Mc-Donald from the nursing home to take her out to our house. Mom would always fix a traditional Sunday dinner consisting of either fried chicken, mashed potatoes and gravy, fresh cut tomatoes if we had them, salad with French dressing that mom made, maybe some cottage cheese that mom made, fresh homemade rolls and cinnamon rolls and then some type of desert; more likely ice cream with her chocolate cake with runny frosting. If it wasn't fried chicken then it might be slow cooked roast, potatoes and carrots with salad and corn. Left over roast, potatoes and carrots became left over beef stew for supper or later in the week. Eating cornbread and beans with fried potatoes were more a week day meal. Oyster stew, potato soup, or salmon patties with fried potatoes and navy beans or creamed corn were normal supper meals as well.

Breakfast was served from 5:00 to 5:30 am during school days so that the cows could be milked, finish our chores, clean up, get dressed and catch the bus by 7:00 am. Breakfast normally consisted of either pancakes with her homemade syrup, bacon or sausage, and a fried egg. Or it might be biscuits and gravy with sausage and a fried egg or it might be biscuits and ham gravy with fried ham and a fried egg. I can't really remember eating much cereal as a kid, maybe a bowl of oatmeal or cream of wheat on cold mornings but rarely dry cereal. If we did have dry cereal it was probably shredded wheat, corn flakes, grape nuts or cheerios. Mom made us hot cocoa from Hershey cocoa and fresh cream and milk.

We raised our own beef and pork so we always had hamburger, steaks and roast, sausage, bacon, pork chops and ham to eat. Sometimes we bought young chicks from the Co-Op or by mail order which we raised to be young fryers. When they got big enough we would pull the chicken's heads off using the heal of my boots and then mom would dip them in boiling hot water to loosen the feathers to make them easier to pluck. We would then pluck and gut them and bag them and freeze for later use. Sometimes we had a hog or beef slaughtered at the farm and processed the meat, but most of the time we would haul them to the slaughter house in Woodward. I remember mom taking the talon or fat from a beef we had slaughtered and render it down into lard to be used for cooking. Sometimes we got lard in five gallon buckets from the processing plant and mom never had to render it down. She used the lard for frying food, making pie crusts or biscuits. We always had fresh eggs to eat from our hens that laid eggs in the hen house east of our house. When an old hen quit laying eggs or a rooster got too mean, they became chicken and dumplings or chicken and noodles. Nothing went to waste around our farm. We raised our own potatoes and stored them down in the cellar. We raised both field and sweet corn, onions, cucumbers, tomatoes and green beans. Mom made dill pickles and relishes and her own syrup that we ate on pancakes. We bought large bags of flour from Jess Ray's Grocery that had to be sifted before baking. The bags themselves had a flower or paisley design on them that mom would save and use for making the girl's dresses.

I kind of had the same arrangement with mom about small game I hunted, as I did with the currants we picked. She told me that if killed any small game that she would fry or cook it for me if I cleaned it. The same arrangement was made for any fish I could catch. Challenge was accepted. I was all the time heading out to the east and west tree rows south of our house to see what I could scare up. The tree rows had a bounty of dove, quail, squirrels and cottontail rabbits in it. It was nothing for me to show up with half dozen of quail or dove and two or three rabbits and squirrels. One time I shot what I thought to be a full size squirrel out of the tree only to find out that it was a baby squirrel. It did not kill her so I brought her back to the house for mom to help me doctor her up. She had several 9oz buck shot in her that we were able to extract and put some

Corona Wool fat "cow medicine" on her wounds. In no time she was up and running around and became my and mom's pet squirrel. I called her Sally and mom used to let her sleep on top of her breast all rolled up in a ball while she sat in her recliner. One night I had gotten up to go to the bathroom and stepped on her crushing her. She had rolled up and slept in my jeans that were lying next to the couch where I was sleeping. It broke both mine and mom's heart that I had killed her. That was the last squirrel I ever shot. I was probably about 11 years old.

In addition, to separating cream, churning butter, cleaning the cream separator and cooking, mom somehow found time to sew for us kids and even crocheted afghans for people. She made doll clothes for my sister's baby and Barbie dolls. She made dress from printed flour sacks for my sisters or from material she purchased at Holland's 5 &10. Mom's talent never ceased to amaze me and I didn't think anyone could ever match her talent until I met my wife, but that chapter is yet to come.

Mom loved Christmas time but probably the most special Christmas she had was the year that Larry got to come home early from Vietnam. She used to try to make Christmas special for each of us kids and I remember her hiding our gifts in the dugout down in the basement of our house one year. Belinda, Willneta and I had discovered that this was where she hid the gifts so we knew what we were going to get that year before Christmas day. Other times she would hide the gifts in the boy's bedroom closet or linen cabinets or maybe up in the closet that separated her and dad's bedroom from the middle bedroom. One year she bought me a Five-Year diary that I wrote religiously in for the first 90 days of 1972. I documented in that diary that I got a radio, five pairs of socks, a leather billfold, two tie clasps, a pair of cuff links, a neck tie, a pair of dress levis, two pairs of cowboy cut levis, a green shirt and the diary itself. Later, I remember finding two pairs of brown jersey gloves in that dugout cubby hole that she didn't find to put under the tree.

The town of Vici always gave out bags of candy, fruit and peanuts down at the City Hall. Mom would take us kids to town so that we would get a bag. It always contained chocolate vanilla drops, hard ribbon candy, other hard candy, an orange, an apple and the rest of the bags were filled with peanuts in a shell. Santa Claus was there and I think it was him that handed the bags to us. I think a lot of years, my cousin Niles Young played the part of Santa Claus.

Mom had her lady friends that belonged to the Jolly Webster Club and they would either meet at the old school house south of our house, or at different women's houses about once a month. They would bring different cooked items and desserts for everyone to eat.

And then there was the "party line", the precursor to Facebook, used by all of the neighbor women. The party line was the best thing for spying on your neighbor ever invented. It consisted of 8 households being tied into the same telephone line and each household had its own unique ring. The neighbors on our party line consisted of us, Noble and Ola Johnson, Luther and Hazel Brown, Uncle Earnest and Aunt Lucy Larison, Howard and Elsie Harper, Leo & Ima Jean Helmick, Loyd and Martha Helmick, and Eldred and Olive Ray. Our number was 7F2 and our ring was two short rings. Every household knew their own unique ring but in the case of a long general ring, anyone could answer. It was nothing unusual to pick up the phone to make a call and someone would already be on the line. So you would either interrupt if you had an emergency, listen in on the call, or hang up and wait until they were done. Now mom and Mrs. Johnson loved to listen in as most women did on the party line. Listening in on the party line was as good as watching "As the World Turns" on TV. As the old saying goes "Telephone, telegraph or tell a woman." But to be honest, my dad was just as guilty as the women for listening in on neighbors talking on the party line. Not all people had telephones at this time, for instance my Grandpa and Grandma McDonald never saw the need for one and never had one installed.

Mom was one of the toughest women I ever knew. She suffered from obesity, arthritis, congestive heart failure, a bad gall bladder and later uterine cancer that would take her life. We think she probably had cancer a couple years before she finally had it diagnosed because of rapid weight gain, and by then it was too late. She never complained and just continued trying to do for others rather than herself. She was the most unselfish woman I ever met.

These were the parents that I looked up to and that molded me into the man I became. I would like to think that I learned from both and exhibit traits from both. I still love gardening and growing fruit trees and I love to cook and make some of the same things I remember my mom making, like jellies, jams, cakes with runny frosting, chocolate popcorn balls and blarney stones.

Left: Daddy in 1921 working in Oklahoma gasoline refinery
Right: Daddy and George Seaburn cutting timber in Oregon in 1920's.

Mom, Dad holding Charles with Barbara and Billy in 1948.

CHAPTER 4

Our Neighbors

Life on the farm was hard work but I would not give it up for anything. We had lots of neighbors who lived nearby and by nearby I don't mean like next door but more like a mile or two from us.

To the east we had Leo and Ima Jean Helmick and their two girls Debbie and Diane and son Don. They only lived about ¾ of a mile. Ima Jean was a housewife who was always baking good deserts to eat and from time to time my mom would take Belinda, Willneta and me over to visit, as she would show mom her latest Avon perfume catalog in hopes mom would buy something. She would also babysit Willneta and me if mom got in a pinch and had something to do. Leo was a farmer like dad but also an auctioneer at the Woodward Livestock barn or if someone was holding a public auction he would bid away until everything had sold.

Leo's brother Lloyd Helmick had gone to Alaska with my dad in the 1940's during World War II to help build air fields and highways. Lloyd and his wife Martha lived a couple of miles south of Leo and Ima Jean on another sandy farm which was fit for raising watermelons. Both daddy and Lloyd raised huge black diamond watermelons in the sandy soil but Lloyd also raised a yellow-meat melon that looked like a black diamond but never had the sweetness in my opinion. Martha worked at Pierson Chevrolet as a bookkeeper or secretary keeping the salesmen in line. Lloyd was a farmer like his brother and daddy but he also worked for the Dewey County as a road grader, who would grade the dirt roads when they got too rough, because at that time there were few asphalt county roads in our area.

East of the Helmick's lived the Schamburg's, Loyd "Skeet" and Arlene and their three kids, Sherri, Fred and Monte. Sherri was a year younger than Belinda, Fred was in Willneta's class and Monte was a year younger than me. Skeet was a cattle rancher and had taught science classes at Vici, but had quit teaching shortly after I started to school. Fred and Monte were the closest in age to me and they loved to play baseball, especially Fred who went on to play college ball at NWOSU at Alva. Monte and I used to ride horses together.

South of the Schamburg's place lived Edwin and Mary

Johnson. Edwin like Lloyd Helmick also worked for the county, but he worked for Woodward County driving a dump truck in addition to farming. Mary was a housewife and one of mom's best friends. They had a lot in common because the Johnson's had children in the same grades as some of my siblings. Their oldest son Larry Johnson was in my brother, Larry's class and their daughter Edwina Johnson was in Belinda's class. Their middle son Donnie Johnson was somewhere in between the two.

Edwin's mother and father were our nearest neighbors to the west or up on the hill as we would say. Their names were Noble and Ola Johnson and their bachelor son Leonard. Noble was seven years older than daddy being born in 1890 and Ola was a year younger than daddy being born in 1898. Noble died in 1969 from pneumonia when I was nine years old. He is one of the first deaths I remember as a young kid. Leonard lived at home with his mother and helped take care of her. Mrs. Johnson, as we called her was another one of mom's closest friends and we visited her often. She had an old chicken bucket that she kept toys in for Willneta and I to play with and we knew where she kept it. There was kind of an opening in the wall by refrigerator that the bucket fit into and whenever we came over we immediately went for the opening, pulled out the bucket and played intently and let mom and Mrs. Johnson visit or gossip. Leonard farmed their place but also worked in town at the Vici Co-op in the feed mill.

Back to the south of the Johnsons lived the old couple Earnest and Lucy Larison. They were both in their nineties when they died in 1974, she was 95 and he was 93. Both of them had lost their first spouses and remarried one another. I remember them celebrating their 25th wedding anniversary. We called them Uncle Earnest and Aunt Lucy, though they really were not our uncle or aunt. Uncle Earnest and his first wife Grace were original homesteaders around Vici when my Grandpa and Grandma Young came to the country. Uncle Earnest was two years younger than Aunt Lucy, but he was about a foot taller than her. He was about deaf and she was about blind. They were quite the pair, but my dad was always lending a hand or a kid to help them out if they needed fence repaired, hay hauled or chores done. My oldest brother Billy lost part of a finger helping pull pipe out of Uncle Earnest's windmill. I remember their coal burning potbelly stove that they used to heat their little two bedroom house and the small separator room which was detached from the house where they separated cream from the milk. They had a big peach tree right next to the house that I used to eat peaches when they were ripe. Later, before they died, Uncle Earnest's nephew, Dale Larison and his wife Kaye came to live on the farm and help Uncle Earnest. Rumor has it that Dale was not really his nephew but his son. Sad thing was that Dale came back to Vici to help Uncle Earnest by building new fences and revamping the old farm, but when Uncle Earnest died before Aunt Lucy, Aunt Lucy's heirs got the farm and Dale was left out in the cold. He would later commit suicide in 1975, leaving Kaye a widow. He was a good man that I admired dearly.

Living back to the south and west of Uncle Earnest and Aunt Lucy were two of mom and dad's dearest friends Edgar and Jean Shaw. Edgar really was a nephew to Uncle Earnest. His mother was Uncle Earnest's sister. Edgar and Jean had three living children, Janice who was a year older than my brother Charles, Jerald who was the same age as Charles and Roger who was a couple years younger than my brother Larry. Edgar raised hogs and cattle and always had a big garden. He was also a carpenter and built the kitchen cabinets in our house. My brother Charles was his assistant and learned how to build cabinets from helping Edgar. Edgar had served in the Navy during World War II and loved to tell his tales of the Navy to his teenage boys Sunday School Class, that both Charles and Larry attended every Sunday in the basement of the Nazarene Church in Vici. Jean was a housewife and a good cook. I remember going over to eat supper at their house with mom and dad one evening and Jean brought out some brandied peaches. I think this was my first time I had tasted alcohol or at least something that was fermented. And to think they were good Nazarenes like us belonging to the same church.

Further to the west of the Shaw's lived John and Beulah Cook. They had two boys, Tommy and Timmy and a couple of daughters, Nancy and LaRay. My brother Charles was kind of sweet on LaRay who was in the same class and the story goes that one evening he took her, my brother Larry and my first cousin Leroy Killough to see a drive-in movie at Woodward. He came back to our house to let Larry and Leroy out before taking LaRay home. Larry being the prankster he was pretended to get out of the back seat of the car, but instead stayed in and hid in the floorboard. Charles proceeded on to LaRay's house, but before they got to the Johnson place Larry raised up out of the back seat and put his arms across the back of their seat until they finally noticed him there. Needless to say Charles was not pleased, made a U-turn and took Larry back to the house, this time to get out.

Back to the east of the Shaw's lived James and Opal Lynes. James was a small man that always used horses and mules to farm. He liked to butcher animals and would come to your farm to slaughter and butcher hogs. Opal was kind of a mean woman, as I remember her and us kids hated it if mom chose her to babysit us.

A couple miles west of us lived Cecil and Linda Guthrie. They actually lived on the Young homestead place where my grandparents had settled in 1916. They had two children Teresa and Troy Guthrie who used to ride our bus route. They were younger than Willneta and I.

Back to the north on the same road was the Stevens' place. The only Stevens that lived on the home place, when I was little was Clayton, who died in 1982, though his brother Jim farmed the place until he died by a farm accident in 1983. Martha Helmick was one of their sisters. There were over 12 Stevens' children, but I think most of them have passed.

Further west down the same road and living back to the south were George and Cora Lea Altland. George was a farmer and cattle rancher who raised good alfalfa hay. In fact that was who my Grandpa MacDonald had bought hay from the day he was killed, when driving back to his house. Willneta and I loved to visit the Altland's because Cora Lea had a large Santa Claus doll collection that ran on batteries that would move or blow smoke through his pipe. George loved his chewing tobacco and he would bite off a piece from his plug tobacco bar and chew on it and barely spit. However, I do remember him having a brass spittoon by his chair. He was a big man and had white hair, as did Cora Lea and we always questioned it they might be Santa Claus and Mrs. Claus when we were little kids.

North of them lived Merle and Marla Guthrie. Merle worked for Woodward County and ran the road grader that graded our dirt roads. He was a cattle rancher and later we sold him our west 80 acres that daddy had purchased across for the Young homestead. They had two boys and one girl. Craig was just a year younger than me and Lynn a couple years younger. Their daughter Christina was several years younger than me.

Back to the north of the Stevens lived the Brown's. Originally this is where Luther and Hazel Brown lived, but later Luther's son Jackie and his wife Mildred moved back to Vici with their three sons Joe, Larry and Martin. The Browns milked cows and sold their cream like us. Joe was two years younger than my brother Larry graduating in 1970. Larry and Martin Brown both graduated in 1972, a year before Belinda. If we needed help, the Brown's would volunteer to help us do chores and we, likewise. Jackie worked at the Farmer's Co-op in the feed mill with Leonard Johnson our neighbor up on the hill.

Further north of the Brown's is where my Uncle Check and Aunt Fannie lived. Uncle Check always had cleaner and nicer vehicles than us. His pickup didn't have any dents and his Chevrolet car looked new. He kept both parked inside a garage shed just north of their house. Aunt Fannie was a meticulous housewife who kept her house clean all the time. All of their kids had been gone for years and they were retired farmer and housewife who took very good care of their property. Uncle Check had a 3010 John Deere tractor while we had just purchased a 2510 John Deere tractor. Daddy and Uncle Check had several pieces of farm equipment that they bought jointly or with other neighbors and we would share the equipment when needed. I remember a hay elevator used for putting hay bales in the barn lofts was jointly owned by Uncle Check, daddy and George Taylor. I think Uncle Check, daddy, Urban

Weaver and Jackie Brown jointly owned a manure spreader and daddy and Uncle Check might have jointly owned a John Deere square hay baler.

Back east of Uncle Check lived George Taylor whom we shared the hay elevator with and then further east of him lived Lile and Dottie Mae Mote. Lile's dad Bernard Mote place was back to west of George Taylor and back south and butted up to our North 80. Lile's oldest son Duane and his wife Shirley lived in that house. Our place was originally owned by Bernard's brother Carl and which daddy bought in 1947. Bernard and his brother Carl Mote had ordered their homes from Montgomery Ward probably back in the 1920's and they had the same floor plans. We figured the barn on our home place was built around the same time as our house.

These were all of our neighbors that lived a 2 to 3 mile radius around our farm. As you could tell most of our neighbors had a second job to help support their farm income, as none were rich from farming alone. Those like my dad, Uncle Check, George Altland, George Taylor and several others who did not have second jobs were older and probably already drawing their social security checks to help supplement their farming income.

CHAPTER 5

Our Town

We lived near the town of Vici, Oklahoma, a small town in Northwest Oklahoma. It has two main highways that run through it, State Highway 34 that runs north and south and US Highway 60 that runs east and west, which is Broadway. Where the two highways intersect, we once had a red light hanging over the street, but it was later taken down and two stop signs put up on the north and south side of the streets to stop north and south-bound traffic but left open for east and west bound traffic. The town was established in February 1899 when Albert Vincent received a permit to establish a post office two and one-half miles southeast of the present Vici site. He served as postmaster, and the mail came from Beement, six miles east. Vincent soon moved his post office/store to a spot three-fourths of a mile south of present Vici, and another store was moved there from Beement in 1902. That was the beginning of "Old Vici." More businesses followed, including a hotel, and then a school. On May 10, 1908, a tornado blew away the entire town, and the townspeople all huddled in a cave to take cover. There were no injuries, and residents quickly rebuilt their homes and businesses. The *Vici Visitor* was printed weekly in 1906, followed by the *Vici Beacon* in 1911.

Vici is located in Dewey County and is 21 miles south of Woodward, Oklahoma on State Highway 34, and 10 miles north of Camargo, OK on the same highway. It is 21 miles west of Seiling, Oklahoma and 23 miles east of Arnett on US Highway 60. It sits atop a hill and lights on top of the grain elevators of the Vici Co-op act like a beacon at night, seen for miles from all directions. It is a small farming community that grew in prosperity as an agricultural shipping point during the 1920s, 1930s, and 1940s because of the Missouri, Kansas, Texas railroad (Katy)that ran through it. In fact it was the railroad that caused business owners to relocate Vici from the old site to what was now called the "New Vici", which a town plat was filed on Sept. 11, 1911. Other businesses like a hardware store located in Cestos, Oklahoma also moved to New Vici" to take advantage of the railroad.

The population of Vici grew from 425 in 1920 to 617

in 1940. After World War II the population declined but by 1960 had grown back to 601 people inhabiting the small town. Ranching, oil and gas activity, and a large nursing home provided the economic base in the late twentieth century. Although rail service ended in 1972, the town grew to 845 residents by 1980. Vici maintains a mayor and town board form of government. The 2000 census recorded 668 residents, and the 2010 census counted an increase to 699. Iochem, a Japanese owned company that produces iodine from the brine solution of oil and gas wells around the town, now provides a major source of employment for local town people and has helped to save the town from dwindling in size, like some of the communities surrounding it.

Back when I was growing up the Vici schools consisted of grades 1-12. There wasn't a kindergarten class until 1969 or 1970 when the school added a new north addition that included the kindergarten class room, an elementary Principal office, a teacher's lounge, a new Cafeteria, a reading room, a secretary office and Superintendent's office and a band room. Prior to the north addition the school looked pretty much like an "H" with the elementary school classes 1-6 being on the west side and the Junior and High School classes 7-12 being on the east side with the auditorium in the middle to fill out the "H" shape.

Broadway of Vici was lively when I was a kid. We had a total of four grocery stores at one time. Ray's Food Mart, owned by Jesse and Bessie Ray was where we did our grocery shopping the majority of the time. Their store was located on the south side of Broadway near City Hall. Their son Eldred Ray helped them run the store. On the north side across from Jess Ray's was Milford Stowe's store located next to the old Post Office. Further down Broadway on the north side was Bud's Grocery and Meats, ran by one of my best friend's parents Bud and Joan Salisbury and then Best Way Foods several stores down from Bud's, ran by Rhea Moore.

The Bank of Vici operated by Glenn Trimble, Jr. was originally located on the northeast corner of US Highway 60 and State Highway 34. A new Bank of Vici was built in 1972 and was located on the north side of Broadway west of the old Post Office. The old Post Office would later be relocated to the north side of town off of State Highway 34, about one block off of Broadway.

The old Fire Department station used to be located south of the hotel, next to the water tower, but a new building was built just north of Hollands off of Highway 34 after I had graduated from high school.

We had several cafes or restaurants located on Broadway. One was Emery's Café ran by Emery and Juanita Moss but it closed sometime in 1968 or 1969. The next restaurant I remembered was the Dairy Land, which was run by Henry

Thompson. This was our favorite pit stop about once a week when our bus driver, Dick Turner would drop us off and let us buy a dairy treat to eat on the bus. Later the Dairy Land would be purchased by Dave McCleery and he would expand the size of the restaurant and call it the D&K Café. This is where my sister Willneta worked as a waitress during her high school years. About the same time Emery's Café was operating on the South side of Broadway there was another café called the Sunrise Café on the north side of Broadway. Prior to it becoming the Sunrise Café it had been the only bakery in Vici. Later it would be torn down and be called Eastman's Café and later the Vici Restaurant. It was originally owned by George and Jeri Eastman and it was built in 1970. It has changed hands several times since its existence and at one time was ran by Dixie Salisbury. It is the only restaurant still operating today and still serves good home cooked meals. In the middle of the restaurant are a string of long tables with chairs, called the liar's table, where you were welcomed to pull up a chair and participate.

At one time there were as many as five separate gasoline stations in Vici. Currently, there are only three operating and one of those did not exist when I was a kid. James Andrews ran the Phillips 66 on the east end of town. He had an ice house that sold big blocks of ice and had an ice crusher outside the house used for crushing the ice and bagging it up for customers to take home and use. We stopped by there most Sundays to purchase the ice required for making homemade ice cream. James sold the 66 station to Leland Kennedy for a few years before taking it back over in the middle 1970's. Across the street and east of the Phillips 66 was Hilbert Coulson's Champlin Station and tire store. My dad used to purchase tires from Hilbert for our car and pickup. One time daddy asked Hilbert why the tires he was purchasing were not lasting as long as he thought they ought to. Hilbert's reply was, "Well Willis, if you came uptown on a Saturday night, you would see why they aren't lasting". You see, my brothers Charles and Larry were taking the 1964 Impala to town and drag racing on most Saturday nights, pulling over truck drivers out west of town with the bubble gum police light Charles bought to put on the cab of the car with a suction cup. Plus Charles had installed a full blown police siren under the hood of the car that sounded like a real police siren. Then further west there was a Conoco station next to Pierson Chevrolet, which is still there today. It was owned by Jerry Bailey and then by Richard Harris for about one year then Melvin Halderman for several years before he sold it to Melvin and Beverly Sweet. They would operate it as Sweet's Short Stop for over 30 years before it changed hands twice more and is currently call Longstops owned by Cliff Coleman. Then there was the Farmer's Co-op filling station where we usually bought our gas because daddy could charge it to his account at the Co-op. When I was a kid, you could buy full size candy bars at the Co-op for a nickel a piece, or six for a quarter. I always looked forward to going to town with daddy and spending a quarter on 6 candy bars. Later on the Co-op station located by the feed store would be closed and the Co-op purchased the Phillips 66 station from James Andrews and that is where it is located today. The other gas station that I really don't remember was west of Milford Stowe's Grocery on the corner of that block where the Bank of Vici is now located. My brother Billy told me about this one, so I am not sure when it went out of business.

We had a hardware store ran by Dale and Ada Allen next to the old Bank of Vici. They sold everything from nuts and bolts to rifles and shotguns. Story goes that one year Charles and Larry bought daddy a Thorsen ratchet and deep socket set for Christmas. Later daddy got the bill from the Hardware store for the boys having charged the tools on daddy's charge account. I guess the thought was what mattered. I bought my first .22 rifle from Ada when I was 14 years old, a Winchester Model 290 semi-automatic. I still have that gun today. Then when I turned 16 I bought my Winchester Model 94 30-30 deer rifle from Ada Allen. That's where I used to buy most of my ammo for my 12 gauge and 410 shotguns and the two rifles. But sometimes I would buy shotgun shells at the Co-op feed store that was across from the filling station or over at the Western Auto.

Jim Stevens ran the Western Auto and tag agency just off

of State Highway 34 on the north side of town. His son Bruce has since ran the business after Jim was killed in a tragic farm accident out on the Stevens farm near our home place.

We had two clothing stores in Vici, one was Holland's Department or as we call it Holland's 5&10 ran by Frank and Stella Holland on the corner of US Highway 60 and State Highway 34. Stella Randolph worked there and she would always make a fuss over Willneta and me when we came in with mom. It was our favorite store to go to besides Jess Ray's Grocery across the street, because they sold everything from Clothes to toys. Mom used to buy patterns and material in there for making the girls dresses. Willneta and I loved it because they sold penny candy and toys. Once, Willneta and I stole some penny candy from there. Why we did it I do not know, we probably had the money to pay for it. This would be the only thing I ever stole from a store and it still convicts me to this day that I did it. We used to buy Styrofoam airplanes, kites, Frisbees, super balls, jacks, Slinkies, play dough, etc. from that store. Back then Belinda, Willneta and I got 1/3 of a monthly Social Security check from dad's earnings, since he was drawing Social Security and we were under 18 years old. I think when it was just us three the check amounted to about $100, or roughly $33 a kid. So each month we had to use that money to buy any clothes we needed and the rest we could spend on what we wanted. The other clothing store was the Vici Dry Goods, owned by George and

Violet Turner. They sold clothing like shirts, blouses, dresses and slacks, Levi's and Wrangler jeans, coats, boots and shoes for both adult and children. I always bought my rough out boots there and my Levi jeans and cowboy shirts using the money I got from Social Security. Marie Moss the grandmother of Dianne Moss, a girl in my class worked in the Vici Dry Goods and she was a sweetheart to me along with Violet Turner. They were both great women.

We had two drug stores and one Sundries stores in Vici when I was little. One was called Carter's Drug Store ran by Mr. and Mrs. Carter. This is where we bought all of our school supplies like Big Chief writing tablets, pencils, erasers, Elmer's glue, Crayola Crayons, folders and binders. They also sold firecrackers during 4th of July. Mr. Carter died in 1965, so I really don't remember him so much but I can still visualize Mrs. Carter today. Dwayne Brown would later move to Vici and open Brown's Pharmacy on the south side of Broadway next to John's Barber Shop. His wife opened the Vici Flower shop next to the pharmacy giving Vici a much needed flower shop for funerals and special occasions. Then there was Holland Sundries owned by John and Ann Holland. Ann Holland was Dr. Young's nurse. Around 1973, the Hollands would sell the sundries store to Josephine and Denver McAlary and renamed it McAlary's Sundries. It was next to Bud's Groceries and was run by Josephine McAlary. Now she was the sweetest lady and loved to feed us school kids who opted to not eat the lunch-room food. I walked from the school almost every day with a couple of other buddies to eat at McAlary's. She had frozen cheeseburgers with Canadian bacon on them that she heated up in the microwave or convection oven. I ate one of those plus a chocolate milk shake every day before going to Bud's Groceries next door and loading up on 6 candy bars for a quarter just like the Co-op. And I wonder why I got so fat back then. My sister Willneta worked several months for Jo McAlary after she got married and while her husband Kerry was working out at the refinery west of town.

Alvin Baker, my friend Junior Salisbury's uncle, owned Baker's Furniture and Electric located on both the south and north sides of Broadway. Alvin sold everything from dining room sets to bedroom sets, sofas and recliners to riding lawn mowers and air conditioner units. His main show room was on the south side but a lot of his inventory was on the north side next to the Vici Hardware.

There were several beer joints in Vici and a pool hall/ domino parlor. Harry and Jo Lively ran Lively's Tavern the beer joint on the south side of Broadway and when I was probably 15 years old, Kenny Campbell and I would go in there during our lunch hour and shoot pool on their 6 foot pool tables. Harry and Jo Lively's son, Don Lively ran another beer joint out north of town by the city park. It was called Lively's Way and also had gas pumps. It was a combination convenience store/ beer joint. This is where I usually filled up with gas and would buy my beer later on. Ralph Kygar had the pool hall/ domino parlor on the north side and instead of the standard 8' pool table, he had a 9' snooker table. My friend Danny Salisbury was quite the pool shark and snooker player. He was also a pinball wizard on the pinball machine in the old Dairy Land. Donita Nix ran another beer joint on the east side of town next to the laundry mat.

When I was 17 I was in what they called the VAOT program at school which allowed you to go to school from 8:00 to 12:00 and then find employment in the afternoons. Sometimes instead of going to work for a farmer that might not need me that day, I would instead go to Donita Nix's beer joint and drink beer all afternoon. I used to write checks to her on my checking account. Some of the checks got rejected by the bank because they could not make out my signature. True story. One day I drank from 12:00 until about 7:00 that evening and then got in my third car, a 1968 Oldsmobile Cutlass that had the engine from my first car and the air shocks from my second car with chrome mag wheels and 50 tires on the rear end. It looked like a muscle car. Anyway I was drunk and trying to show off my hot rodding skills, so I revved up the car threw it in reverse and then was going to throw it into drive and leave black marks over by James Andrews Phillips 66. Before I got it thrown into drive I hit James's gas pump behind me, pushing one of the pumps backwards. All of the sudden liquid was shooting up in the air. I thought it was gasoline, but fortunately, for me it was only the water hydrant next to the gas pump that had broken off and was spewing water into the air. Robert Day, James's nephew worked for James and he was there and said that he had already shut off the fuel pumps when they closed around 6:00. Needless to say, my folks were not happy about what had happened and neither was Wayne Cunningham, our Farm Bureau insurance agent. Daddy got a letter in the mail saying that I could no longer be covered on any of his vehicle policies and that my coverage was cancelled on my vehicle. That's when I became a State Farm customer in 1977 and still use them today for most of my insurance needs.

There was the Vici Drycleaners on the corner next to Ray's Food Mart and in between that was a beauty parlor owned by the same people that owned the dry cleaners. Going down the street south and across the alley was Rupert Vaughn's Shoe repair and upholstery. Rupert was Jean Shaw's dad and the only shoe repair shop in town. His grandson Roger Shaw would later take over the business after he died and his son Otis Clay Vaughn would run the upholstery part of the shop.

Across the street from the Vici Dry Cleaners was the Dobson Telephone store and then next to it was The Vici Auto Parts that worked on cars, trucks, and motorcycles. Wendell Jones owned the shop and his wife Jackie was one of my Sunday school teachers at church. You could order automotive parts there and he sold chainsaws and motorcycles. This is where Charles bought his first motorcycle that daddy made him take back.

George Harbison ran a Harbison Heating and Plumbing Company just east of Alvin Baker's and next to Jo and Harry Lively's Beer Joint. The real brain of heating and cooling though was Paul Steinmetz, the father of one of my classmates, Mary Steinmetz. He was considered a genius around town. His daughter Mary was our class Valedictorian while I was the Salutatorian.

We had one lumber company located north of the Farmer's Co-op owned by an old man that lived to be 102, just about 6 weeks shy of turning 103. His name was Russel Nixon. I can remember going there to buy 1"x8" lumber boards and 2x4s for building cattle panels with daddy. Most other building supplies we would purchase at the Co-Op Feed store. It carried nails, steeples, leather gloves, fence stretchers, come-a-longs, electric fence post, insulators, nuts, bolts, veterinary supplies, livestock feed, etc.

We had one doctor in Vici and maybe one Chiropractor. Dr. James Young had the corner office just east of Rhea Moore's Best Way Foods. He was no relation, but one time I did get a check made out to Jim Young in the mail that was a payment for services rendered. Needless, to say I did not get to keep the check. We hated to go see him as he would always give us a shot for this or that ailment, or maybe they were just vaccine shots. Nonetheless, this was not my favorite place to go and I can still taste the wooden stick he would place in my mouth and tell me to say "aww". Billie McAlary, one of Larry's classmates worked for Dr. Young and she would always make a fuss over us because I think she liked Larry. I am not sure what Dr. Meyers was but I think he must have been a chiropractor and he lived next door to the City Hall building.

We had one hotel in Vici owned by Orval Care that was located on the corner on the south side of Broadway. It was a two story building that burned down about 15 years ago leaving a vacant site on Broadway. We had one Motel owned by Avis Moss called the Deuce of Hearts Motel, just east of Pierson Chevrolet on the south side of the street. It has since been torn down and Savings and Loan Company was built on that location.

We have had several barbers come and go over the years but when I was a kid I remember Toby Baker, Junior Salisbury's grandpa and Alvin Baker's dad being on the north side of Broadway and John Salisbury, Junior's uncle being on the south side of Broadway. Spud Castor used to cut hair with John before he retired. Spud was an old timer around Vici and for some reason he had volunteered to be our chaperone on a school trip to the Zoo in Oklahoma City when we were 6th graders. Us boys had found a Playboy magazine somewhere and were looking at the articles in it on the bus. Spud noticed that we were looking at something interesting so he came back and busted us. He took away the magazine, I guess to look at the articles as well. John cut my hair from the time I was little until well after I married and he even cut my two boys hair if we went to Vici to visit mom in the 1980s. He was a good man and I looked up to him and his brother Bill Salisbury who was my Vo-Ag instructor in high school. When I was about 11 years old I decided to save the $2.50 it cost to cut my hair, so I tried cutting it myself with a set of clippers used for show steers. Needless, to say my self-inflicted haircut was a disaster, so I had to go have John straighten it out for me. He asked me what happened and I quickly conjured up a story that my brother-in-law Joe Maddox had tried to cut my hair. I think John was to the wiser and knew I was the culprit, but he did his best to repair the damage and I never tried that again.

Alice Hale had a beauty salon north of the Vici Restaurant. I think it was built at the same time the Vici Restaurant was built in 1970. Alice was married to Vestal Hale who was the brother of Geri Eastman one of the owners of the restaurant. Alice and Vestal had four children that rode our bus route. Rex the oldest was in Belinda's class, Randy the next oldest graduated in 1975, then Rene was in Willneta's class with Rena Jo being two years younger than me.

Pierson Chevrolet was the only car dealer in town. They occupied a showroom, mechanic shop and body shop on the south side of Broadway with a car lot on the north side of Broadway. My first cousin Niles and his son Mickey would later build the Young's Body Shop building west of town, which is now owned by a distant cousin Eric Morris who does automotive repair. Mickey would relocate the Body shop to where Wendell Jones used to have his automotive shop. Charles Campbell would build his own automotive repair shop out west of Vici on his farm and that's where we normally took our vehicles for repair. Both Niles Young and Charles Campbell originally worked for Pierson Chevrolet before starting their own business. Richard Dryden also ran an automotive repair shop on the north side of Vici and I used to go help him work on my second and third cars when something would go wrong with them. He liked to drink beer, so I would sit on a bench and drink beer with him when I was 16 and 17 years old, while helping him work on my cars.

My Uncle Albert Bowman was the only blacksmith in town at that time. He had helped built our broom corn wagon used for hauling watermelons, our sled used for stacking hay straight off of the baler, built our stock racks used for hauling cattle and hogs to market or slaughter, and built side boards for our pickup used to haul wheat or cow feed. He also built some sideboards for Charles's 1963 V-6 GMC pickup when he moved to Florida. Uncle Albert was a big man and had fought in World War I. He was married to my Aunt Freeda and they lived just north of the Lumber Company. I would always get volunteered to help Aunt Freeda pull up her sweet corn stalks after the corn had been harvested for the year. She made the best skillet fried corn. Uncle Albert loved kids and built an electric merry-go-round next to his shop that had 4 or 5 seats for kids to sit in and then he would turn it on and around and around we would go. I remember the big anvil in his shop and the coal burning forge he used to heat and bend metal and make things. That's an art that has truly gone to the way side.

While Uncle Albert was an old blacksmith, my cousin Everett Hutchens was a welder and he had the only welding shop in Vici at the time called Everett's Welding and Repair. He built everything from cattle guards for farmers and ranchers to hay and grain feeders, cattle panels, working shoots and anything else you might want fabricated and welded together. His son Buddy and his grandson Bob Hutchens now runs the shop and his daughter Leann helps with the family business. Sometime after I had graduated from high school, Leann's husband Bill Key would open a second welding shop in Vici called Key's Welding.

Vici Farmer Co-op Grain Elevators

CHAPTER 6

My Early Years

My earliest recollection or memory thinking back would probably be eating watermelon on the tailgate of a pickup parked under a mulberry tree in the front drive of our farm house. I would be sitting there in shorts with no top on and watermelon juice dripping down my round belly. I think to this day, this is why I cannot stand to get sticky. The knife used to cut the watermelons was an old hickory handled butcher knife that had been sharpened so many times that he it had a curve to it in the middle. Mom used the same knife for cutting up chickens to fry.

My next earliest recollection would have to be when I was about three years old, or in 1963 and I remember going with mom Belinda and Willneta to Woodward to pick up daddy at the bus depot. He evidently had traveled out to Idaho to look at the farm he was going to purchase and move us to Idaho. I don't remember us selling our farm northwest of Vici, but according to my brothers he had sold it but after seeing the place in Idaho, he changed his mind and was able to get the sales transactions voided on our farm. I guess he had sold the Antis Place (240 acres) and the south home place (80 acres) to Leo Helmick. He had sold the home place or north 80 acres to Lile Mote and he had sold the west 80 acres to someone in Woodward. Larry remembered being excited about the opportunities of moving to what he thought was Bend Oregon, but my brother Billy said it was around Wendell, Idaho rather than Oregon. Billy said that daddy was trying to convince him and Wanna to move out there with us. Billy and Wanna would have just been newlyweds in April of 1963. Daddy told him this farm was big enough that it could support both our family and Billy's.

When I was about 4 years old I remember the big fight in our dining room between my dad and my grandpa McDonald. Now there was only five years difference in their ages, my dad being born in 1897 and my grandpa being born in 1892. I remember sitting on the brown bench in our dining room when they started yelling and shouting at one another and then the fist started flying. The fight then went outside, as my brothers Charles and Larry remember seeing them fight under the mulberry trees next to the house. Larry remembered daddy picking up a two inch diameter limb broken off one of the trees to use on grandpa, but he said that he never did use it on him. Larry thinks the fight started over grandpa bringing up daddy selling the farm the previous year and that daddy blamed mom for us not moving out to Idaho. Billy thought the fight might have started over something Dale, mom's brother had done. He said that daddy did not like Dale because he was always in trouble and was no good. I just know that as a little kid, the fight scared me and I learned from this fight not to let myself be caught in the same situation around my kids and later my grandkids.

I was about 5 years old on March 7, 1965 when we decided to go see Grandpa and Grandma McDonald who lived about 6 miles east and 1 mile north of us. Charles was the designated driver of our 1961 Chevrolet Impala. Belinda didn't go with us but instead was at the Helmick's playing with Diane. Larry and our neighbor Jimmy Brown were riding horses back off of the same road we were traveling on. Daddy did not go, so it was just Charles, Mom, Willneta and I that went. We were about half way there when we met Greg Pierson, son of one of the Pierson Chevrolet owners on a sandy hill top. We ended up having a head-on collision which threw Mom, Willneta and I under the dash of the car. Charles was holding so tight to the steering wheel that it bent the wheel and made an impression of the wheel into his chest. Willneta had her face cut up real bad and a broken arm. She still has a scar on her face today from the wreck. I suffered a broken left leg just above the knee and had cuts to my face and nose. For years I could still feel small pieces of glass try to protrude out of the skin around my nose. My broken leg required a plate and four screws to hold the femur bone in place. I had to wear a cast on my entire left leg from the thigh to ankle and a partial cast on my right leg with a bridge attaching the two casts together just above the knee. Mom was shoved up under the dash of the car with her knees, so that it made it almost impossible to get her out of the car. It injured her back and hip. Belinda remembered that mom and I did not get out of the hospital until March 23, 1965 which was one day before her 10th birthday. It was determined, that neither Charles nor Greg was at fault for the accident, so the insurance paid off and we got a used 1964 Chevrolet Impala after the accident.

This was my first incident of breaking a bone but would not be my last. I learned how to live with a cast that did not allow me to walk and that scratched after several weeks from the hair that grew under it on my leg. Dr. Jack Fetzer was our doctor who would cut off the old cast and x-ray the leg on every visit until the cast came off permanently. This wouldn't be the last time Dr. Fetzer would treat me for broken bones. The cast he built made it easy for daddy to pick me up and carry me around until I was finally fitted in a cast that allowed me to use crutches. Having a broken leg really limited me from having much fun and I remember still being in crutches when my 5th birthday came. I think I also remember getting the mumps while being bed ridden with the broken leg. I think Willneta's arm healed quicker than my leg.

Willneta and I always had a fascination for fire and matches. We used to go on the north side of the house and burn the grass next to the house or burn the grass around the propane tank. Little did we know that we could have blown ourselves up.

I used to take the propane torches we used to heat up the vacuum lines on the milking machines and burn spider webs in the barn. I would even go up in the hay loft and burn spider webs that hung over the milking stanchions. I was just lucky I didn't start a fire in the dry hay we stored in the loft.

I was probably about 6 or 7 years old when I was helping my brother Larry milk the cows. We always had cats in the barn and there was a cute little yellow tabby tom cat that couldn't be more than a couple months old. Larry had just poured milk out of the milking machine into one of the 10 quart pales and sat it on the bench. The little tom cat had been observing what Larry had done and decided to go get some milk for himself. He jumped and caught the side of the pale with his claws and pulled himself up to get a drink when Larry spotted him hanging onto the pale. Larry picked up a club and hit him in the head killing him instantly. He was jerking on the ground with blood coming out of his ears. I screamed at the top of my lungs "You killed him", and ran off to the hen house east of our house. I hid up in the loft of the hen house. I liked to have never forgiven Larry for killing that kitten.

When I was probably 9 or 10 I went to get the cows to milk in the north pasture. I had some matches in my pocket. As I passed by an old hay feeder in the north pasture full of love grass hay I decided to see if the dew on the hay would keep it from burning. I lit a match and put under some of the wet hay and it started smoking a gray black smoke. Before I knew it, the fire began to burn a bright orange yellow flame and then the entire contents of the hay started burning out of control. I ran to the house and told mom who called the volunteer fire department in Vici. She was so excited that she told them the fire was 3 miles north and 3 miles south of Vici. They questioned her again and got the right directions of 3 miles north and 3 miles west of Vici. It took the firemen several hours to put out the fire and it was the talk of the town and at school that day. Daddy was so mad at me, and needless to say I had learned my lesson about starting fires.

CHAPTER 7

Life on the Farm

MILK COWS AND HORSES

The year was 1968 when I probably started really helping out on the farm. I was eight years old and was expected to start contributing to the tasks of running a wheat and dairy farm. My chores back then probably consisted of retrieving the milk cows from the north 80 early in the morning and bringing them up to the barn to be loaded into the milking stanchions, four at a time. But first I probably had to bring two 2-1/2 gallon buckets of warm water from the house to be used for cleaning out the electric milking machines and cleaning the cow's teats and udders. Then I would scoop out half a gallon of feed from the feed bin in the barn and put in each of the stalls where the stanchions were used to lock the cows in place for their milking. Some of the warm water was used to clean the cow's teats before attaching the vacuum suckers on them. The milking machine was electric and created an air vacuum motion that sucked and released, sucked and released the cows teats until milk started flowing into the collection bucket hooked up to the milkers. A black rubber hose ran from the milkers to a valve on the galvanized airline coming off of the air tank connected to the electric motor. After each cow was milked the collection tank was emptied into 2-1/2 gallon galvanized pales to be taken back to the house to be run through the cream separator.

Some cows had so much milk that we might have their calves and some additional calves we purchased to help milk them dry. Usually we would be milking two cows in the two far north stanchions while nursing calves on the two cows in the two south stanchions. We milked anywhere from 7 to 14 cows every morning and evening depending on when the cows calved. Every cow had a name that we milked. There was May the only Holstein we had, Guernsey the only Guernsey we had, a Brown Swiss that I can't recall her name and then we had our milking shorthorn cows, which made up most of the herd. There was Star, Red, Lady, Lilly, Roanie, Rosie, Tiny, and Patty, just to name the ones I can remember.

Tiny, one of the milking shorthorns, was the cow I liked the most. She would let me jump up on her back and lay there and sleep while waiting to put the next group of 4 cows into the milking stanchions. One time while dad was milking Tiny she kicked dad across the barn into the north wall. She must have had a sore udder or something because she was one of the tamest cows that we milked. Needless to say, daddy did not take getting kicked lightly and he proceeded to beat Tiny with one of the rubber hoses used for suction.

We kept the cows in the north pasture after the evening milking, so that is where I had to retrieve them in the dark most mornings before going to school. In the mornings after we milked all of the cows we would release them out of south gate of the corral next to the large concrete water tank they drank from. We would drive them across the road to the south tree rows where they could go all the way back to the Antis place for grazing during the day. Then that evening I would ride my horse Star out to the south pasture to retrieve them for the evening milking and so went the process of rotating them from the north to south pastures every day.

I mentioned using Star my horse for retrieving the cows in the evening. I got Star, a chestnut Welch mare when I was 8 and had her until I turned 15 and had outgrown her. I rode her bareback most of the time but would use an old saddle that Charles and Larry had used on their horse Stoney on occasion when I needed to take my rifle or shotgun with me. Daddy had always seemed to make sure all of his boys had a horse while growing up. Billy told me about his first horse Cyclone who daddy thought was to mean spirited so he bought Billy a horse named Spot. When Charles and Larry came along he bought them a cream colored Mustang called Stoney. When Larry went off to college, he felt like Stoney was too large for me to ride so he bought me Star the Welch pony. I rode her almost every day bringing in the cows and would take her on some of my hunting adventures during dove seasons or ride her over to the west 80 to check on the cattle grazing there. Of course I always used her for our annual cattle drive from the home place to the west 80 and vice versa. She was pretty much my horse but sometimes my sisters and nieces and nephews would ride on her with me. She only had one speed leaving the farm, slow; and one speed coming back to the farm or water tank, fast. She would run up to the cement water tank at a full gallop and just before hitting it, stop abruptly, trying to throw you into the tank. We kept her in the middle of the barn behind where we milked the cows and it was my responsibility to feed her and take her up to the tank twice a day for water. If we turned her loose in the pasture with the cows, you could not catch her. She had a tendency to try to scrape her rider off her back by running under the lowest limb on a tree out in the tree rows. Those trees had thorns on them. She would lower her head and then run under the limb hoping to brush you off. Once I took her over to the west 80 to count the cows. I left her tied up to the outside of the fence and went up on an old dam ridge to count the cows. When I turned back around there she was running down the dirt road heading back north and then back east to the house. I cut across Gene Altland's pasture and the Johnson place trying to catch her but she beat me back to the barn. I learned to never let go of the reins if she did buck or scrape me off as she would run away. One other time I was riding Star out in the corral playing a little game of chase with the new Hereford bull that daddy had bought that had kind of a mean streak in him. That bull hated Star and it became a game to see if we could run by the bull without him getting us. One time Star and I did not judge our timing correctly and he got us that time. He picked up both me and Star with his head and shoved us into the west corral barbed wire fence. Star drug me for a little ways and my left leg got a long cut on the calf of it. Of course to make things worse, mom was looking out the west kitchen window and saw the whole thing. She came running out of the house screaming at the bull and then at me for teasing him. She bandaged me up with some old torn sheets she used for wound care and put a glob of "cow medicine" in the wound after she cleaned it out. Seems like this may have been the same bull that rolled daddy while leading him to water.

Daddy would give each of us younger kids our own cow that we would get the calf born to her that year. My cow seemed to always have a still born calf so I never got a calf for several years. Finally, I asked if Tiny could be my cow since she was my favorite. Later, I would start to build my own herd of brahma cows from a calf I bought at the sale barn. Her name was Della and her first heifer calf was Sally. I ended up selling them both after I went to college and that was the end of my cow herd. Of course, I always had show steers while growing up that daddy and Mr. Taylor helped me pick out.

Picture of the barn we used to milk cows

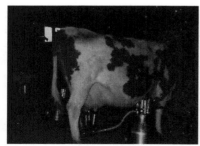

Milking cows and nursing calves

FEEDER HOGS AND SHOW PIGS

I was probably more of hog man than a beef man. There was something about hogs that appealed to me and they seemed like easier money to make than cattle. I remember a sow had a litter of Chesterwhite or Yorkshire pigs and there was one runt in the litter. I made a pet out of him and he used to follow me and actually come up to our back porch and knocked on the door. I think I called him Arnold after the pig on "Green Acres", a popular sitcom playing on television at the time.

I tried my luck farrowing litters of pigs from a couple of sows, but found out that was not as easy as it looked. We did not have good facilities or farrowing crates like the Turner's or Shaw's did so I lost a lot of pigs from the sow laying on them. I decided instead to buy feeder pigs and raise them to butcher weight of around 200-240 lbs. I gradually increased my hog operation to where I was feeding out 30 pigs at one time. Before I got to this stage of operations, I asked dad if I could use the pig pen on the south side of the road and he told me I could if I rebuilt the fence around the entire pen area. I agreed and started working on the project when I was probably 11 or 12 years old. Dad had cut some fence posts out of the tree rows. I used the posts that were stacked and he bought some new hog wire and barbed wire to attach to the posts with steeples. He showed me how to make a fence stretcher out of two 2x4s to keep tension of the hog wire evenly and how to build braces for the four corner posts and two gate posts. While I was building the pen and stretching the barbed wire, the fence stretchers lost their bite and the barbed wire shot back on me cutting both of my hands. Mom and dad were not home at the time so I jumped in our pickup and drove over to Dennis Turner's house and had Geraldine, his mom bandage up my hand. I was probably 12 years old at that time, but knew how to drive the pickup.

I finally completed the project and bought my first set of feeder pigs from either Don Parry or Edgar Shaw and I was in the hog operation. I do remember trying to farrow two more sows under the corrugated tin building that was located in the center of the pen but after losing too many pigs I became quite content just raising feeder pigs. We still had a smaller pig pen on the north side of the road by our cow tank that I used to pen up my show steers and show hogs.

I had a Hereford steer one year as a show steer and a Yorkshire barrow as a show hog. I would put a halter on the show steer to lead him around and when he would not move, the show hog would bite him on the dew claws and make him follow me. It was the darnedest thing I had ever seen.

In Vo-Ag I built a new corrugated tin building out of 1 inch square tubing and corrugated tin. I sectioned it off with hog panels made out of 1 inch tubing and hog panels and made swinging gates to let the hogs in and out. Dad even sprung for a waterline that crossed the road that ran from our pump house on the north side to my hog waterer on the south side. I bought a 72 gallon hog watering tank from Co-Op and a large used pig feeder from Edgar Shaw. I built hog troughs out of old hot water tanks that I cut in half during Vo-Ag hour and welded angle iron to the bottom of them to keep them from rolling. When Charles moved back in 1977 we rebuilt the old dilapidated hog shoot for loading out the hogs in a pickup and stock racks. We never had a hog or cattle trailer for transporting livestock; just a pickup with the stock racks that Uncle Albert had built to slide in the back of our pickup.

When we had a load of cattle that needed to be taken to market, daddy would normally hire Leo White to come out with his cattle truck or Henry Thompson with his cattle trailer. Steers or heifers and hogs that we had butchered in Woodward, were hauled in the pickup.

Upper: Farrowing Chesterwhite sow with piglets
Lower: Show hog and feeder pigs that I raised and sold

SLEDDING AND HAULING HAY

Our farm consisted of probably 150 acres of either prairie grass fields, love grass fields, alfalfa fields or cultivated land used for producing hay like sowed feed hay or rye and vetch hay. Daddy and uncle Check had traded in the John Deere twine baler for a new Massey Ferguson baler that did a much better job of tying the hay bales with twine rope. Dad had Uncle Albert build what we called a hay sled that could be attached behind the baler and one of us boys would sled hay. The sled was made out of probably a sheet of 1/4 inch metal with a slit cut in the center up to about 2/3 of sheet, then a two-inch pipe was welded to the sheet in the front which had a curve to it like a sled. A chain was welded to the pipe and clevis was attached to the chain in the middle which was then attached to the baler itself. You would catch each individual bale as it came out of the baler and stack it on the sled, three bales on each level for the first three levels and then one bale on top making a stack of ten bales to then be picked up by a pickup for hauling back to the barn or haystack. It beat picking up single hay bales out in the field.

I don't know how many square hay bales I have bucked in my short life on the farm from 8 years to 18 years but it has to be in the high 40 to 50 thousand. In my prime years of 15 to 18 years old, I could haul around 500 bales a day by myself using a pickup. When I was 16 and 17 I worked for Bill Phillips from Sharon, Oklahoma who built a hay wagon out of an old International wheat truck. Boy was that a slick machine. He could drive it and lower a shoot in the center of wagon that had a chain drive with hooks that would catch the square hay bales and convey them up the chain that ran all the way to the back of the wagon. In the center of the wagon was a steel alley with angle iron on both sides to keep the bale running straight. I would catch each hay bale as it came to me and stack them starting at the back and work my way forwards until the hay wagon was full. I think I probably only stacked the hay four bales high and by the time the wagon was full we had close to 200 hay bales on board. Then when we got to the hay loft, all Bill had to do was raise the shoot up to the door of the hay loft and reverse the direction of the chains so that he was sending a steady stream of hay bales to me in the hay loft. Boy could you work up a sweat stacking hay in an unventilated hay loft on a 100 degree day outside, with it feeling like 150 degrees inside the hay loft.

Now we never got paid for sledding or hauling hay for daddy and most of the time daddy put up hay on shares, so not only did you get to haul our hay but you also had to haul the other guys hay. I did hire out and haul hay for other farmers like Leo Helmick, Duane Mote and Wendell and John Turner, but most of the hay I helped sled, haul and stack was for daddy and whoever he went on halves for swathing the hay, normally Bill Phillips or Marion Darden.

Of course there was good hay and bad hay for sledding and hauling. The worse hay by far for hauling and stacking was the love grass hay, which was very slick and hard to stack without the stack collapsing or bales falling apart. Alfalfa was probably the dirtiest hay to sled and one of the more heavy hay bales, but probably the most nutritious of the hay. Sowed feed bales were very heavy but always made nice stacking. Rye and Vetch hay was very nutritious for the cattle but it too was pretty heavy and dirty to sled behind. Prairie grass bales were probably one of the lightest hay bales to haul but would be full of sandburs so you needed to wear hay chaps when hauling it. A few times I would find a prairie rattle snake baled up in the hay bale. Wheat straw bales were the lightest hay bales to haul but probably the worse nutritional value of all of the hays mentioned.

CROPS WE RAISED

The main cash crop we raised was wheat which could be used for grain to be sold or used in our feed. My dad gave me the 7 acres on the northeast corner of the Antis place as my own wheat field that I got whatever wheat it produced. Some years it might produce 30 bushels per acre or 210 bushels of wheat. I normally stored my grain in the farmer's Co-op so that I could use it for making hog feed or for cash if I got in a bind. This was daddy's way I guess of paying me for my labor on the farm, that and getting one calf a year from my cow. We probably raised around 100 acres of wheat off of our 400 acre farm each year. Some years if daddy thought we had or he thought we were going to have a wet year, we would plant sowed feed, rye and vetch, oats or milo for hay or the grain. We had an alfalfa patch south of our house used for hay and another one east of the house that we baled. The field west of our barn on the north 80 was used for growing sowed feed or rye and vetch while I was helping daddy farm. The west field on the south eighty next to the old school land was either planted in wheat, milo or sowed feed. The field south of the east tree rows was where we planted our watermelons but we also planted part of it in milo some years and wheat other years. The Antis place is where most of our wheat land was located. It had a sandy hill that daddy knew how to plant to avoid wind erosion. We always plowed and planted east to west on that hill so not to lose it during a dirt storm and drought like we had in 1977 and like Oklahoma had back in the Dust Bowl days of the 1930s. Daddy was a conservation type of farmer that had learned to respect the land and Mother Nature. The younger farmers who bought that land later after daddy had passed learned the hard way and about lost that hillside. There was a large love grass field on the Antis place and we usually had a haystack of love grass just off the love grass field for feeding cattle during the winter. The rest of the Antis place was pasture and sage brush for running cattle during the summer. Our west 80 was nothing but shin oak native grasses and sage brush where we took our cattle in the spring after the shin oak had bloomed, so it did not kill our cattle. They would graze on it during the summer and then we would move the cattle back that fall before the shin oak turned red.

OUR FARM EQUIPMENT

We were by no means well to do farmers when it came to farm machinery. Our oldest tractor was a 1936 Farmall F-20 that you had to have 6 arms to drive and operate the equipment attached to it. It had a hand throttle, hand brakes, steering wheel, and hand levers for raising and lowering the attachments. The only thing that wasn't hand controlled was the clutch. Billy believes this tractor had belonged to George Braudrick and mom before George committed suicide. We had another Farmall F-20 that might have been a 1937 model that Larry said we bought for parts from Hank Williams. The next tractor we used was a 1943 Farmall Model H gasoline tractor that daddy usually left a cycle bar mower hooked up, used for cutting hay. Charles would later use this same tractor and connect a buzz saw to the PTO wheel for cutting firewood. Then we had a 1948 Farmall Model M gasoline tractor and a 1952 or 1953 Farmall Super M that ran on LP gas or propane. It was not until 1971 that daddy would buy a tractor that had power steering, a 1967 John Deere 2510. That tractor actually had an umbrella shade to protect you from the sun. We had an 8' one-way plow, a 6' three bottom moldboard plow, an 8' tandem disc, a 10' graham hamney chisel and later a 12' Krause chisel with roto tiller attachment. We had a Massey Ferguson twine hay baler, an old steel wheel hay rake and a 20' broomcorn wagon used for hauling watermelons and an old manure spreader, jointly owned by several farmers. Later, daddy would make a trailer out of an old Ford pickup bed. We put sideboards on it and used it for hauling wheat.

The pickups I remember having were a greenish blue and white 1964 Chevrolet, a 1971 White and orange Ford F-250 and then a brown 1974 Chevrolet V-6. I learned to drive a stick shift by driving the 1964 Chevrolet and the 1974 Chevrolet. The 1971 Ford F-250 was an automatic with a 390 engine. I had put Charles's police siren in that pickup for calling in the cattle for evening milking time. It was the best pickup for hauling hay but could get stuck on a wet cow turd or in the sand because of the high speed rear end. That would be the last Ford daddy ever bought.

*Upper left: 1943 Farmall Model H with cycle mower and 1936 Farmall
F-20 with cultivators attached
Upper right: 1952 or 1953 Farmall Model Super M pulling watermelon wagon
Lower left: 1967 John Deere 2510 pulling John Deere wheat drill
Lower right: 1943 Farmall Model H with buzz saw attached*

GARDENING AND WATERMELON PATCHES

We had about three main fields or garden areas on the
farm. The smallest of these gardens was directly west of our
corral up near the water tank. In it we raised smaller vegetables
like onions, tomatoes, cucumbers, green beans and okra. It was
closer to the water hydrant by the water tank so we could water
it with a circular water sprinkler welded to a 1 inch galvanized
pipe. The sprinkler pipe was about 3 feet tall and had a spear on

the bottom to stab it into the ground. I think maybe Charles had built that sprinkler. This was the garden that I was usually in charge of planting and hoeing amongst my other chores in the spring and summer. The next garden area was east of the house and next to the blackberry bushes. Here we always planted a 100 pound sack of seed potatoes. Daddy would sit out on the front porch or under the shade of the mulberry trees dicing up quarters of seed potatoes to make sure each dice had an eye in it to grow a potato plant. Daddy would then load up the potato seeds in a gunny sack and we would head for the garden which was probably 100 feet long by 200 feet wide. He would hook a three bottom mold board plow on the Model M Farmall tractor and cut the first furrow. I would then come behind with a bucket full of seed potatoes and plant them in the furrow. When I was done then he would run the plow again and fill in the furrow I had planted full of seed potatoes and make the second furrow. We would repeat the process until all the seed potatoes were gone. He used to tell me to plant the potatoes 6 inches apart but I would cheat and plant them more like 3 inches apart so we didn't have as many rows to hoe. Next we would plant corn using a hoe that daddy made a furrow. He would tie some baling twine to two stakes for making a straight row, cutting the furrow by following the baling twine. Or if I was lucky he would hook onto the old lister planter that would plant the corn behind the tractor. If we did it the hard way, which is the normal way daddy liked to do it, then I would come behind daddy making the furrow with his hoe and spread 2 corn seeds about every 6 inches. We would normally plant anywhere from 10 to 12 rows of sweet corn. When the potatoes were ready to dig, daddy would hook up to the 3 bottom mold board again and cut the furrow so that the potatoes turned up and came to the top. My brother-in-law Joe Maddox and my nieces and nephew would come down with him to help put the potatoes in gunny sacks. Daddy would always give Joe and Barbara about half of the potatoes we raised. The other half we stored in the cellar.

On the south 80 we had a sandy patch of land that grew great black diamond watermelons that we sold to grocery stores or neighbors, who came by and saw them on our broomcorn wagon parked under the shade trees. Most of the melons we raised weighed from 30 to 45 pounds and were just a sweet as can be. We would clean out the barn about once a year by pitch fork and load into manure spreader, owned jointly by 4 or 5 farmers. Then daddy would spread the manure out in the watermelon patch and disc it into the sandy soil with a tandem disc. He would buy a can of powder snuff tobacco from Bud's grocery and soak the watermelon seeds in water and the snuff to give the seeds a good coat of snuff. He said the snuff would deter the moles and gophers from eating the watermelon seeds before they could germinate. We would then plant about 100 hills of watermelon which was generally about 4 or 5 rows of watermelons with each hill having 20 to 25 hills each. Each hill would get about 4 or 5 seeds in it, to later be thinned out if all five survived. The rows were probably 200 to 250 feet long but seemed like a quarter of a mile when we hoed the pig weeds and Johnson grass out of the watermelon patch. One year daddy decided to plant field corn next to the watermelon patch and he planted 23 rows of field corn. I was 11 that year and my sister Belinda had gone to Red River, NM to help watch the kids belonging to the people who ran Trego's Western Wear. Daddy told me if we got all 23 rows of corn hoed that we could go on vacation to see Belinda. That year the Johnson grass was ridiculous and it seemed like it took forever to hoe all 23 rows, but we did and we got to go on vacation.

HUNTING ON THE FARM

On the south 80 we had two tree rows planted in the 1930s, during the dust bowl days. The majority of the trees planted back then were hedge apple or bois d'arc trees that were a very hard wood with thorny branches. Squirrels loved to build nest in the trees and there was an abundance of dove, quail and cotton tail rabbits. When I was only 9 years old and not doing chores in the fall you would find me hunting the tree rows with a single shot bolt action Springfield 410 shotgun. You only got one chance with a single shot unless you could unload and reload quickly, so I tried to make every shot count. I loved the thrill of the hunt and the sound of a quail taking off in front of you that scared you half to death. I must have shot 400 to 500 shells through that 410 shotgun before I convinced daddy that I was ready for a 12 gauge shotgun. He finally gave in when I turned 12 years old and he took me to Gibson's at Woodward, where I bought my first shotgun for $86. It was a Mossberg 500AT pump shotgun that could shoot either a 2-3/4" shell or a 3" shell. I was in hog heaven. The stock on it was nothing fancy and had no designs, so when Charles came back one time he put a checkered design on the pump and stock of the gun and refinished it with a darker stain. It was beautiful and would kill many quail, dove, and rabbit. I would not shoot any squirrels after stepping on my pet squirrel.

When I turned 14 I bought my first rifle, a Winchester Model 290 .22 LR from Ada Allen for about $50, and then when I turned 16 I bought my first deer rifle, a Winchester Model 94 30-30 for $64. I used to take my 12-gauge shotgun and .22 rifle with me on horseback to hunt dove in the fall. The draws on our wheat field east on the Antis place would have small mud puddles following September rains. This made the perfect habitat for dove to come flying in to water in the evenings. I would be lying on a ridge overlooking the draw with both guns. I would try to pick them off with my .22 LR when they landed and when they took off flying I would try to hit them with my shotgun. I missed more than I hit but I had a blast doing it.

After I got my 30-30 deer rifle I went on my first deer hunt out on the Cree Ranch, west of Vici with my friend Danny Salisbury. We took my brother-in-law Bill Carter with us who told us that if a deer jumped up in front of him, he would not have buck fever. He had no more uttered those words when a buck did get up in front of him and he took off shooting and jumping over brush like a fool. We just laughed at how quickly buck fever hit him. My next deer hunt with that rifle would be with Charles over at the Baptist Assembly Grounds. Charles had a Springfield 30.06 deer rifle with a scope. He lined up on a large buck and shot him. The buck went down slowly and since I was not a seasoned hunter like Charles I went charging towards the buck rather than letting it die. The buck got up and started running on pure adrenaline. We never found it that day or the next and it would not be found until about a week later. It was a huge 10 or 12 point buck and Charles never forgave me for spoiling his hunt.

When I was probably a junior in high school, I had some friends, Junior Salisbury and Russ Cole, come out to the farm. We got my brother's long bow out the gun cabinet and decided to practice our archery skills. Larry had some broadhead arrows in his quiver so we went out in our front yard. Mom's 1974 Caprice was parked on the west side of the yard. We took turns shooting Larry's long bow and when it was Junior's turn to shoot he aimed the bow up into the sky and let the arrow go. The arrow went higher and higher and then started falling back to earth. We ran for cover only to hear something go thud. We turned around just in time to see the arrow sticking straight up out of the hood of my mom's car. It had pierced the steel hood and was directly over the air breather cap of her engine. Of course mom just happened to be looking out the kitchen window and saw what happened. She came running out of the house screaming at me. Junior sensing that he had been caught red handed tried handing the bow off to Russ and then to me. When Russ or Junior and I get together, we still laugh about that incident.

Another funny story I tell was when I was probably 13 or 14, I sent off for some blow guns that I ordered from a Guns And Ammo magazine. There was some type of special if you ordered more than one, so I ordered three and about a thousand blow darts. I was so excited when they arrived in a long cardboard box that was over 5 feet long. After all the blow dart guns were 5, 6 or 7 feet long. I ordered three of the five foot ones. There were not 1,000 blow darts as I expected but instead strings of orange 38 caliber plastic beads and hundreds of long pieces of wire in the box with the blow guns. You had to pull the beads off of the string, cut off a piece of wire to your desired length, heat up one end of the wire and insert into the bead to make your own blow darts. I don't know how many of those darts I made but it must have been the whole 1,000 beads that came with the guns. Mom would catch me in the kitchen with one of the cooktop burners on high, heating up pieces of wire and sticking it into the bead which would let off an awful burned plastic smell. I had the entire house stinking. I learned how to shoot those blow guns pretty good. I used to shoot barn swallow birds coming out of the barn and had a couple that flew around with orange beads coming out of their wings. One time I shot a cottontail rabbit. I had a pretty long blow dart and the blow dart went all the way through the rabbit and pinned it to a tree. One time Joe Thomas came over to play at our house and we went down to the basement. We had cans of peaches on the shelves down there and I shot one of the blow darts all the way through a can of peaches. Then we started being boys and shooting blow darts at one another. I shot one right into Joe's butt cheek when he shot one in my leg.

Picture of tree row I used to hunt

FUN ON THE FARM

Life on the farm was not all work and no play. We had fun as kids on the farm. We played baseball in the front yard with Joe and Barbara and their kids and our star outfielder Snoopy who could actually catch a baseball in the air and bring it back to you. We played Annie Over and Red Rover and hopscotch, jacks and threw a Frisbee to one another and to Snoopy who could catch it in mid-air. We buried old coffee cans in the side of the hill between the Helmick's and us and pretended that the coffee can was our mail box to send notes between us and them. We put hedge apples in the middle of the road to watch neighbors like Leonard, Jackie, and Clayton run over them. We used the barn roof as an object to reflect fly balls and then catch them as they came rolling back off of it. We rode Star on Sundays for entertainment and picked wild grapes over on the west 80, walking barefoot through the sandy road. The only thing missing on that farm was a good fishing pond.

We never had a pond on the farm but we did have a huge cement stock tank in the corral that was probably 15 feet in diameter and maybe 30 inches deep. We had two strands of barbed wire strung across it to keep the cows from stepping into it and walking out of the corral. The north side of it faced the barn and corral and the south side faced the road that ran by our house. Each year dad gave me the task of draining the water and scooping out the green moss that had accumulated in the tank during the year. I would scrub it good and then fill it with fresh well water that came from the pump house that was located next to the tank. We had the best well water around and drinking from the water hose was so refreshing on a hot day. It took about 3 or 4 hours to fill the tank but then it was ready for swimming in. If Barbara's kids were at our house they would join Belinda, Willneta and I swimming in the cement tank, careful to not cut ourselves on the barbed wire that ran across it.

Looking back I cherish those experiences of living on a farm and would not give up one moment. I learned to be disciplined and responsible by having chores that had to be done every day and I learned how to care for animals that depended on me. I still have dreams about whether or not I took Star my horse up to the tank for a drink of water that day or not.

CHAPTER 8

My Grade School Years

I remember starting school in the fall of 1966 and having Mrs. Lenhart as our first grade teacher. I got a spanking the first day for running down the hall and right into her stomach. We started out with 11 kids that first year, 8 of which became 12 year grads attending grades 1-12. There were four girls and four boys. The girls were Carrie Badley, Mary Steinmetz, Penny Smith and Connie Woods. The boys were John and Junior Salisbury, Dennis Turner and myself. Dennis Turner was my best friend for years. Charles had graduated that spring and had gone off to college at Panhandle A&M at Goodwell, Oklahoma. I think I probably got to move into the boy's bedroom with Larry after that.

The second grade we had Mrs. Ila Gregory as our teacher. She had taught all of my brothers and sisters prior to me. I remember her being a good teacher, but none of those teachers took any crap off of the students back then. We were taught to respect your teachers and mind them or face the consequences like I had with Mrs. Lenhart the year before. I started the second grade the fall of 1967 through the spring of 1968, the year Larry graduated. That year I was learning how to milk cows and help do the chores, as Larry was getting ready to go off to college himself at Northwestern Oklahoma State University at Alva, Oklahoma. Charles had already enlisted in the Navy and had completed his basic training and was living in Jacksonville, FL expecting their first baby.

My third grade year's teacher was Mrs. Nina Barney, she too had taught a lot of my brothers and sisters. I remember being afraid to ask if I could go to the bathroom one day and ended up peeing my pants. It was so embarrassing. I think Mrs. Barney had to call my mom to bring some dry clothes. All of the kids laughed at me.

My fourth grade year was a very memorable year as I turned nine in June of 1969 and shortly after we started school in September we went on a Nazarene church wiener roast out at Ila and Carl Bailey's house. They went to our church and had two sons, Neil and Scott. Scott was a year older than me and in Willneta's class. He led a bunch of us boys on a path above one of the canyons that existed on their place. So happens a tree root was sticking up in the middle of the path and when I came running through there I tripped and broke the same leg I had already broken when I was 4 getting ready to turn 5 in 1965. Dr. Fetzer said that my femur bone had broken into right below the plate he had placed in my leg in 1965. He warned me that if I broke that leg one more time, they would just have to saw it off. That scared me to death thinking I might lose my leg and I took him serious trying to avoid breaking that leg again. Again, I found myself in a cast that went from my left hip down to my ankle. I had to miss about 6 weeks of school that year. My teacher was Mrs. Georgia Allen and she used to come out to our house and teach me individually. That same year we took state tests to measure our efficiency in reading, writing, math and science. I remember her administering the test to me out at the house. After the tests were graded she brought back the results and told my mom and dad that I was near a genius for my age. I was always good in school and never considered myself to be any smarter than anyone else so maybe she was just flattering my parents.

On June 29, 1970 my grandpa McDonald was killed returning from George Altland's from getting a load of hay. My dad finally went to see him at the hospital before he died. They had not spoken to each other for about 5 years after having that fight in our dining room. I'm not sure if they made up before Grandpa died or not.

The next year was my 5th grade year and we had Mrs. Donna Clem as our homeroom teacher. She was an excellent teacher and taught us how to write in cursive penmanship. In September of 1970 we got to go to Chicago, Illinois on an AMPI (America's Milk Producer's Incorporated) convention trip. My dad took me, Willneta and Belinda on the trip with him. In addition, the Campbell's out west of Vici went on the same trip. We rode in the back of their pickup camper to catch the airplane in Oklahoma City to Chicago, Illinois. We stayed at the Conrad Hilton downtown Chicago and got to go see some neat museums and Lake Michigan. My dad had his wallet stolen while on the trip. Larry had come home on leave from the Army while we were in Chicago and we missed seeing him before he was to be deployed to Vietnam.

This was probably the year that I had another embarrassing moment while doing exercises at PE over in the old gymnasium. We had to do what they called the duck walk, squatting down and walking on our legs bent at the knees. I had brought some Oreo cookies with me and had them in the pockets of my gym shorts. As I would duck walk the cookies would crumble and leave a trail of brown and white all the way down the gym floor. Everyone laughed at me again. That was the year of separating the boys from the girls and giving the girls the big talk about life changing events to their bodies. I remember noticing that the girls' bodies were starting to change and we had a new girl in our class that was more developed than the other girls. Her name was Tammy Bozarth and she was the granddaughter of Henry Thompson who owned the Dairy Land down town. She was very pretty and smart and she was the most talented artist I had ever seen. I thought I could draw back then because I would enter those art contests in magazines that challenged you to replicate a drawing without actually tracing it. But Tammy could draw anything freelance. She put my drawings to shame.

The winter of 1971 we had a blizzard in January or February that made snow drifts 6 to 8 feet tall and we had to use the tractor to get around the farm. We still had our old Model M and Super M Farmall tractors to get around. We did not buy the John Deere until the summer of 1971.

The sixth grade year started in the fall of 1971 through the spring of 1972 and many things happened that school year. That was the year Larry had gone to fight in Vietnam and came back home in December 1971. I got a diary that Christmas and documented events like my Uncle Joe Killough getting killed in a car wreck, Charles, Nina and the kids coming back to see us in January 1972, having another small blizzard in January 1972 but not as bad as the blizzard of 1971. Larry and I took the new John Deere tractor down the road and helped pull out an oil field worker that was stuck in the snow. He gave Larry a fifth of Wild Turkey whiskey for our efforts. I documented the first day I tried to dip Skoal tobacco on January 25, 1972 out in the little building by our ball field across from the elementary school. I had found an old can of dried up Skoal that Larry had left in his old FFA jacket I was wearing to do chores. I couldn't understand why guys liked dipping this crap so much. I later became an avid dipper of Skoal and Copenhagen. I documented the day daddy got rolled by the bull and snoopy saved him. I wrote down that Billy brought his 1961 Volkswagen Bug over to our farm for storing until he could come get it in the spring. On March 4, 1972, I decided to take ole Herbie for a ride and headed west and then back to Uncle Earnest and Aunt Lucy's house. I drove around their circle drive and then instead of going back home I decided to turn west out of their drive and go around the section mile. I got Herbie up to 55 MPH and then the sandy road west of Uncle Earnest's place got me. I started fishtailing and going from one side of the road to the other and eventually lost control and rolled the bug, landing on top of Uncle Earnest weak barbed wire fence. It landed on its wheels on top of the fence, so I jumped out to see if I could pick it up and lift it off of the fence. It was too heavy for me to lift even with all the adrenaline running through my body. The top was caved in and battery acid was running out of the battery which was now up in the front seat where I had been sitting. I took off running back east to Uncle Earnest and Aunt Lucy's place to call our house but no one was home. I scared Aunt Lucy to death when I came running up to their door and knocked. Uncle Earnest had already lost his driver's license and could no longer drive so they could not give me a ride back to our house so I started running back home. When I got there daddy had just got home and I told him what happened. Needless to say, he was not happy with me and cussed me all the way back over to where I had wrecked. I think we cut the barbed wire and pulled the bug back onto the road and daddy pulled it back to the house behind the pickup with me steering the bug. Joe Mack and Teresa found out about me wrecking Herbie and they were mad at me for quite a while. Billy ended up selling Herbie to Paul Steinmetz and never did take it back to Evergreen, Colorado.

That same year we had Mr. Burns as our homeroom teacher and science teacher. He gave us an assignment to build a model of any kind of bridge over the weekend. Just happened that this was the same day daddy had been rolled by the bull and we never had any good paint to paint my bridge. All I could find was some old white oil based paint that was clumpy and thick. I did my best with what I had and turned in my bridge that next Monday. Mr. Burns gave me a C on the project while my best friend Dennis Turner made an A on his. You could tell that Geraldine, Dennis's mom had done an excellent job building Dennis' suspension bridge out of old thread spools and twine. I explained to Mr. Burns that we were not able to go to town to buy good paint for painting my bridge because daddy was laid up with pleurisy from being rolled by the bull on that Friday February 25, 1972. Mr. Burns was one of Charles' classmate that had come back to teach at Vici. He took pity on me and raised my score from a C to a B-. I remember my Uncle Floyd and Aunt Toots coming to live with us several weeks while daddy was recovering. Our neighbor's boy Larry Brown, who was a senior that year, helped me milk in the mornings and gave me a ride to school rather than having to ride the bus. That spring we had a sixth grade party out at Bill and Nancy Salisbury's house. John, their son and Junior their nephew came up with a fifth of whiskey for us boys to try. I remember taking the bottle and pouring it out. Everyone made fun of me for being such a righteous boy. That righteous attitude would not last long, as I entered my teenage years.

During the spring of 1972, I helped Dale McAlary assemble a 1,400 bushel grain bin on our farm to store wheat. The grain bin had a cone shaped pit formed out of concrete that was about five feet deep. We assembled the bin by putting the top together first then raising it up and adding each additional ring to the bottom until it was done, then attached the bin to the concrete base with bolts. Dale was a patient man and I learned a new skill helping assemble the grain bin.

CHAPTER 9

4-H and FFA

From the 4th grade to the 8th grade I was in 4-H Club where I participated in county and district livestock shows at Taloga and Woodward, Oklahoma. Our instructor was G.W. Taylor who was also our grade school principal. In addition to showing steers and hogs at County fairs and livestock shows, 4-H was a learning experience where we learned the different cuts of meat for beef, hog and lamb. We were challenged to do monthly talks and demonstration in front of the other 4-H students. When I was probably 11 years old or in the 5th grade I did a talk on "gun safety". I brought my .410 single shot bolt action shotgun with me on the bus that morning. Now I was a chubby kid and I got picked on a lot from the older boys on our bus route. Tom Drake was three years older than me, had reddish-brown hair, wore a thick corduroy jacket and smoked in the back seat of the bus every day. He blew the smoke into his coat like no one could see him. He even bragged about the fact that he rolled his own cigarettes in some fancy cigarette maker. He always picked on me and the day I brought that shotgun on the bus I got his attention. I think he thought I had brought the gun to get revenge for his bullying. Dick Turner our bus driver made me leave the gun up at the front with him, once I had explained why I was bringing it to school with me. It was not unusual for high school boys to have guns hanging in the rear windows of their pickups to go hunting when school was out. There were no mass shootings at schools during these times.

I showed quite a few steers that daddy and Mr. Taylor helped to pick from daddy's herd of calves. I learned how to break lead them and make them move their legs backwards or forwards until all four legs were standing at attention for displaying them to the judges. I bought what was called a show stick which telescoped in and out and it had a three point star on the end made out of hard plastic. It was used to place the star in the center of their hooves or behind their dew claws to put pressure on them until they moved their legs forward or backward. We always gave our steers a bath once we got to Taloga and then Mr. Taylor would help us trim their hair and fluff up their tails to make them presentable for showing the next day. Jim Peck didn't like to give his steers baths so he would pay one of us boys to wash his steer. It was easy money.

Jim's dad Vernon, always bought Jim the best steer Nigel Parry had on his registered Charolais farm out east of Vici. We never had that kind of money to spend on a steer so I always settled for a calf out of my dad's milking shorthorn herd. One year I did show a Hereford steer, but most of the time it was a milking shorthorn. My last year in 4-H or 8th grade year, I showed a wild milking shorthorn that ran through a bunch of FFA boys who were helping us break lead our steers. He dragged about 4 or 5 boys trying to keep ahold of him on the lead rope. Eventually, we did get him broke and he was one of my best steers.

When I was probably 13 or 14 I used to let other kids hit me in the stomach for money when we went to Taloga. I could hold my breath and make my stomach hard as a rock and never did get hurt until Mr. Taylor saw what I was doing and he gave me five licks of the paddle that next Monday at school.

Daddy used to go out to the pastures and cut stands of grass for me to enter in the fair at Taloga. He would cut a stack of Big Blue Stem, Little Blue Stem and Indian native grasses and I would win first place blue ribbons or second place red ribbons. He would pick one of his prize watermelons out of the watermelon patch and I would win another blue ribbon.

I loved the fair at Taloga because they had a small carnival with different booths set up to win money or show off your throwing skills. I loved to throw a baseball at the water dunk tank. It consisted of a seat over a water tank enclosed by a steel cage to protect the man or woman sitting on the seat. A steel bar extended from the seat that had a square plate of metal which was the target to hit with the baseball. Once you hit that plate or the bar itself, it would cause the seat to be released sending the man or woman sitting on the seat into the cold water below. I was pretty accurate and dunked many a participant.

I also started showing barrows and gilts at the county stock shows. I would buy them at annual pig sale held at the Woodward Livestock fairgrounds. Jim Steenbergen always had the best Duroc breed pigs but they were too expensive so I either settled for a cross-breed, Chesterwhite, Yorkshire, Hampshire or a Poland China. I would normally spend about $25 or $30 on a pig to show.

Me and my milking shorthorn show steer probably taken in 1971 or 1972 over at Jackie Brown's barn, while in 4-H.

124

Me and one of my milking shorthorn show steers around 1973 or 1974.

From 4-H your transitioned into FFA (Future Farmers of America) when you were a 9th grader. The Freshmen year was the initiation for greenhands. We had to wear a full size onion around our necks by putting a string through the center of the onion. Every time we saw an upper classmen who was in FFA we had to say "yes sir" or "no sir" to him. If we failed to address him correctly, we had to take a bite out of the onion. I remember trying to buy the least spicy type onion, like a Vidalia onion that could be tolerated. Our FFA Instructor was one of my friend's father and another's uncle, Bill Salisbury. All of us boys looked up to Bill and he became a great role model. We took what was called Vo-Ag under Bill, which was a one hour class. We learned all about the different types of grass, grains, cattle, hogs, sheep and farming techniques. We would spend about 30 minutes in the classroom and the remainder of the time out in the shop area where we learned how to weld and use a cutting torch. We built cattle panels, hog sheds, working shoots, hay feeders, hog troughs and grain feeders. If a farmer needed some cattle worked then we would all load up in the back of our Vo-Ag pickup and head out to the farmer's place where we would work and dehorn cattle, work hogs or vaccinate cattle and hogs. I loved this kind of work and enjoyed the excitement of bull dogging a young bull if we did not have a working shoot to run them through. We would come back to class smelling like pig or cow manure with dirt all over our blue jeans. Most of the time when we did go help a farmer work cattle it would take longer than the Vo-Ag hour, but we were excused from getting to the next class late.

My junior year I showed a Yorkshire barrow and won Grand Champion at Taloga which I got a Purple ribbon and a brass trophy with a pig on it. My senior year I got to participate in what they called the VAOT program that allowed me to complete the hours I needed to graduate from 8:00 to noon, but then I could go work in the afternoons. That senior year I worked for Bill Phillips and Junior Baird, two farmers up by Sharon, Oklahoma plowing fields and building fence.

I even worked for my instructor Bill Salisbury one fall applying anhydrous ammonia fertilizer on his wheat fields. His son John was in my class and we decided to cool down a six pack of Coors beer with the anhydrous ammonia gas by spraying the six pack with it. About the time we had sprayed the six pack, Bill drove up in his pickup. We quickly put the six pack in the cab of tractor to hide it from Bill. When Bill got out of the pickup he told one of us to get in the tractor and start it up. The six pack still had the fumes from the fertilizer on it and it made your eyes tear up something awful. Bill couldn't figure out why we were crying. I don't think we ever did get to enjoy that six pack of beer.

During my senior year, Bill Salisbury encouraged me to apply for the FFA State Farmer degree, an award only given to seniors who submitted an application and scrap book which described the activities and farming experiences that we were involved in. There were three of us applying for the award that year, John Salisbury, Dennis Turner and myself. All three of us received the award at the state convention held in May 1978 at Oklahoma State University in Stillwater, Oklahoma. Bill and Nancy Salisbury gave my parents a ride to the ceremony. I had received three very nice letters of recommendation for the award by our Co-op Manager, Joe Rogers, the president of the Bank of Vici, Glenn W. Trimble, Jr. and our high school principal, Cleo Moran. All of the letters spoke to my high ethical and moral standards that I exhibited as a young man. I still have the scrap book and those letters today.

While in Vo-Ag I made a hog shed, hog panels with swinging gates, hog troughs, hay feeders and cow feeders and a working shoot, made out of pipe for working cattle. I loved to weld and make things. Welding is what would later be the reason why I got a job working on the corporate farm where I got injured.

1975 FFA OFFICERS

Back row:
Bill Salisbury – Vo-Ag Instructor
John Salisbury – Sentinel
Russ Boyd – Treasurer
Jim Young – Vice President

Claretta Lingenfelter - Sweetheart
Dennis Turner – President

Front Row:
Milburn Outhier – Reporter
Lynn Evans - Secretary

1978 FFA OFFICERS

Back row: Dennis Turner, Mark Outhier, Jim Young
Front Row:Danny Salisbury, Carrie Badley, John & Junior Salisbury

CHAPTER 10

My Junior High and High School Years

My seventh grade year started in the fall of 1972 and went through May of 1973, the year Belinda graduated from High School. That same year on January 2, 1973, Charles Badley was paralyzed from the neck down when our school bus was hit at the same intersection, where my Grandpa McDonald was killed 3 years earlier. Again, another oilfield worker plowed through that intersection and this time hit a bus half full of kids. I am not sure why we were not on the bus ourselves or if Dick Turner had just let us off and was heading west to drop off students living west of us. Or, it could have been that Belinda was now driving and brought us home from school. Charles was severely injured and would live the remaining years of his life in a wheelchair as a quadriplegic. Little did I know that I would be going through something similar, a short 6 years later.

We had escaped being taught by Mertle Gastineau whose reputation had preceded her and instead we had Mrs. Reed as our 7th grade home room and English teacher. She was a sweet lady and even taught us how to make homemade fudge in her class one day. I still make that homemade fudge from time to time so I do not get rusty. One day in her class I had bought a pair of X-Ray glasses that had little peep holes in the centers of the lens with a red and white spirals all around the lenses. I ordered them from some dirty magazine that I had found or bought and took them to class with me. Our hormones were raging at this time of our life and we were going through puberty. I gave the glasses to Eddie Berry to put on and he was staring at Dianne Moss when Mrs. Reed came in the door and busted him. Everyone laughed at Eddie and then he pointed to me and told her that they were my X-Ray glasses. I think that was the end of the X-Ray glasses, but we had convinced Dianne Moss that we were able to see underneath her clothes, even though we could not.

This would be the year that I started smoking little filtered cigars called Winchesters, that had just came out in 1972 and were packaged like cigarettes but smelled liked cigars. They were so addictive and I got to where I would smoke them behind the barn when going after the milk cows or out in the pastures. I would hide the filters under rocks on the west side of the barn. I got more and more daring about smoking them and eventually started sneaking a smoke in the barn itself, when daddy would take a bucket of milk up to the house or just when I was alone milking the cows. I started throwing those cigarette butts behind the old Gold Spot refrigerator we had in the barn to store cow medicine or vaccines and fly dust. One day daddy said, "You know I think we should clean out the barn and move that old refrigerator and clean behind it." I spoke up quickly and volunteered to clean the barn by myself. Daddy knew what was behind that old refrigerator and was just baiting me to confess, which I never did.

My 7th grade year was a year of initiation by the older boys where they would give you bus riders by pulling your underwear up as high as they could or by giving you twirlies by sticking your head in the toilets and flushing them. We had been the king on the mountain as sixth graders but now we were low man on the totem pole as seventh graders. I kept getting harassed by a ninth grade boy named Lynn Evans every day at lunch. He would pick on me and try to get me to fight him. Finally, one day I got fed up and told him to meet me on the front lawn of the school at noon hour. Everybody gathered around to watch the big fight. Lynn and I went at it, and I threw one lucky blow that hit him right in the mouth. I think he ended up having to get 11 stitches. He had me down on the ground choking me and dripping his blood all over my new purple shirt I was wearing. Some of the sophomore boys,

Monte and Phil Salisbury started calling me pinky and Cassius Clay after that one lucky punch. Lynn's father also called Lynn Evans, who used to be the Vo-Ag teacher before Bill Salisbury was furious and had a meeting with the principal Elwin Randall and my dad and demanded that daddy pay for Lynn's medical bills. After the truth came out that Lynn had been bullying me all year and that I finally put an end to it, his dad dropped the matter. Needless, to say Lynn quit picking on me and we even became friends when we both had to sing in the boy's chorus together.

One of my most embarrassing moments during 1973 was during our end of year assembly where they passed out awards and achievements to all of the students. Belinda had asked me to go get her Perfect Attendance certificate for her. She wasn't there the day to receive it, go figure. I listened waiting for Belinda's name to be called and then I thought they said Belinda's name so I went up on stage to receive it for Belinda. My cousin Linda Young came up to the stage also, and followed me off the stage and said, "Give me my award". Evidently they said Linda and not Belinda. Everyone laughed at me as usual. I was so embarrassed.

The eight grade year was better than the 7th grade as we now had the new 7th graders to pick on instead of us being initiated we were now part of the initiation process. That Year Coach Larry Hawk was our home room teacher. He had been our 7th/8th grade History teacher and the boys Sr. High and Jr.

High basketball and baseball coach. Because I had to milk cows in the morning and evenings, daddy did not let me participate in any after school activities like baseball or basketball. So instead I took PE while the other boys practiced baseball and basketball. PE class was up on the 2nd floor of the gymnasium and there were ping pong or table tennis tables up there, weight lifting equipment, etc. We also played chess during PE hour and of course I loved playing chess and was quite good. Larry had taught me how to play when I was about 6 or 7 years old. I even became a good table tennis player and learned how to put a backwards spin on my serve that was impossible to hit. I may have not been able to play school sports but I managed to stay active on the farm playing catch by myself using the barn roof as my backstop or by throwing rocks from the barn up to the cement cow tank. I threw a long cattle stick like a spear and lifted a piece of railroad iron daddy used as an anvil to build up the biceps in my arms. I used the old refrigerator in the barn as my punching bag putting many a dent into that door.

1974 was Wesley Turner's graduation year and he was kind enough to let me and Dennis ride around with him in his new 1974 Ford F-150 pickup. We rode with him to and from the Taloga County fair getting up to 100 mph, while listening to Wipe Out on his 8 track tape player. This is when I fell in love with speed and hot rodding. That same year Stephen Hutchinson's dad bought him a brand new 1974 or 1975 Gold Pontiac Trans Am with the big Firebird painted on the hood and the honeycomb mag wheels. It was a beauty but would be short-lived for Stephen got in trouble for drugs and the car I believe got confiscated and taken away. That was every young boy's dream car back then. Yes we had drugs back when I was in junior high, being used by some of the older boys but no one in our class had tried them yet, or at least I don't think anyone had. I know I never did ever smoke or take any illegal drugs when I was a teenager and still have not. That's one part of my life that I take great pride in for not falling into peer pressure and making the wrong decision like I had with cigarettes and would later with alcohol.

As I mentioned, Wesley Turner, Dennis's brother was graduating this year and he was given the opportunity to drive one of his uncle's stock car up at the Woodward Speedway. He drove against some of the great driver's from the area like Buck Cadwell, Junior Cadwell, Roger Habekott, Randy Ogden, and our local favorite home boy Tom Jones. Buck drove car #07, Junior drove #44, Roger drove #77, Wesley drove his uncle Jerome Brown's car #4 and Tom Jones drove #68. Tom was kind of a legend around the Vici area as an Evil Knievel on a motorcycle. He could ride one standing up on the seat. It was so exciting to go to the Woodward Speedway and watch the local favorites fight it out around that dirt track from 1974 – 1977.

The summer of 1974 another tragedy struck when my brother, Larry's wife Tonya shot herself on June 16, 1974. This would be the first in-law that we would lose.

The fall of 1974 I entered my freshmen year of high school. It was my first year of high school and I was in FFA and got to take shop, where I learned how to weld, do woodworking and leathercraft. My FFA instructor was Bill Salisbury and my shop teacher was David Clem, the husband of my 5th grade teacher Mrs. Clem. I loved leathercraft and learned how to make belts and billfolds and was soon taking orders and making quite a bit of money from selling them. Mr. Clem taught us how to use hand tools and learn all of the different types of woods, before he let us use power tools and machinery. I thought he was the best shop teacher even though my brother Larry didn't care for him when he was in shop. Charles on the other hand thought Mr. Clem was a good teacher also.

I was showing steers in the fall and the spring of 1975. While we were at the Woodward District Livestock show in March 1975, we got word that our neighbor Dale Larison had shot himself in his front yard. Rumor had it that Dale had been over at town that night gambling and had lost the farm in a poker game. Kaye, his wife found him the next morning in his pickup. He had shot himself in the head with a shotgun. Blood and brain matter were everywhere. Charles must have been on leave and Larry who had just experienced the suicide of his own wife 9 months earlier were given the task of cleaning out Dale's pickup. Larry said that he had never seen anything so bad. Dale was only 52 years old. We all took his death hard, as he was a good man.

It was probably in the summer of 1975 that I drank my first beer and became drunk. Larry and I were doing chores that day for some reason. Mom and dad must have gone somewhere for Larry to be helping me but nonetheless Larry let me go with him in his 1974 GMC pickup that had a 454 cubic inch engine and could really move. We drove around the countryside drinking Coors beer and after a few I was feeling drunk and got sick. Larry told me that I had better not throw up in his pickup and he punched it kicking in the four bbl. carburetor and we went sailing over the old railroad crossing east of our house. I began to throw up in the floorboard of his pickup making a big mess. He got me out at the house and made me go lie down while he cleaned out his pickup with the water hose. Fortunately, he had vinyl seats and floorboards. That would be my first real experience with drinking but not my last. Larry was called Adolph by some of his buddies and I later became known as Little Adolph because of the Coors beer we drank.

It was in 1975 that I sold Star and got a buckskin quarter horse from my 2nd cousin Jimmy Bauers. I had just outgrown Star and needed a larger horse to ride. I hated giving up Star, as the two of us had many adventures and mishaps. My legs were almost touching the ground riding her. Star went to Mendel White a boy that was a couple years younger than me. His father Alvin White was our windmill repair man. Alvin saw me a short time after he had bought Star and asked me about Star. He said that Star would run to their tank with Mendel on his back and then try to throw him into the cow tank. I told him that was just the way Star was and that Mendel would get used to her, just as I had. I only had the buckskin a couple of years and never rode him as much as I did Star. I don't even remember selling him, but Larry thought I sold him to J.C. Buck.

It was probably my sophomore year that I got in argument with my dad while helping him put up an electric fence. We were south of the house up on the terrace above our alfalfa field. Daddy was driving the John Deere tractor on the grass field below the terrace when I decided to pick up a glass insulator and throw it at him. I think he was about 100 feet from me when I launched the insulator into the air towards him. I had no idea that I could throw that heavy insulator as far as I did. It was an old glass insulator used on the telephone lines that we were using for our electric fence. I remember watching the insulator fly through the air towards my dad riding across the grass field when it hit him in the head. I remember him stopping the tractor and looking back at me. I thought I had killed him but he just looked at me in disgust and drove on. I never tried anything like that again and was just glad I did not hurt him. At this time in my life I thought I knew everything.

In the fall of 1975 we were playing football during our noon hour in front of the school when I got the ball and was rushing for a touchdown. Jimmy Joe Kygar was the only opponent in front of me to prevent me from making a touchdown. He hit me and sent me into the one of the steel posts that stuck up to prevent cars from parking on the lawn. The impact caused me to hurt my right ankle. I hobbled around on it all day and my shop teacher Gary Adams told me that it was just a sprain. I did chores that evening and finally my dad said we needed to go to the hospital to see if it was broken. Sure enough it was broken and I got a cast on my right ankle and a pair of crutches to get around.

I was growing my feeder hog operation during this time and had quite a bit of money in my checking account from selling hogs and from making belts. In May 1976 I heard about a 1970 Pontiac Lemans that was for sale. A guy named Fuji Hammond had the car and only wanted $800 for it. It was a Maroon two door with a black vinyl top. It had a 350 cu. Inch engine with a Hurst 4 speed transmission, no air condition-ing and radio/8 track tape player with power booster speakers in the back. I talked daddy into letting me buy the car before I turned 16 in June. I was in hog heaven and this is probably why I quit riding my buckskin horse that summer and ended up selling him. That car had more horsepower than I needed and ended up wrapped around a telephone pole north of Main Street. Again, daddy and I got into an argument six months after buying the Lemans and I would go storming out of the drive nearly taking out the wheat drill parked there. I went to town found someone to buy me a case of beer, bought a couple packs of Marlboro cigarettes and picked up my friend Junior Salisbury. We went to Woodward and picked up Russ Cole and drove around drinking the case of bottled Coors beer. I let Russ drive the car at one time and we went up to his FFA teacher's house and about lost control of the car going down his drive. Then we went back to Woodward and drove down an alley to take a leak when the Woodward police pulled us over and asked us what we were doing. They did not arrest us but told us to get home. We dropped Russ off at his house and then Junior and I went back to Vici where I dropped him off at his house about 1:30 or 2:00 in the morning. I had one beer left to drink so I drank it and was heading north out of town to go home. I shifted gears hitting it hard coming off of Broadway going from 1st to 2nd and then 3rd gear getting up to about 80 mph in only two blocks. I had my window down and was going to throw the beer bottle over my car to hit a sign when I pulled the steering wheel into a hard right turn setting me into a power slide. I took out a stop sign, insurance sign, a corner post, two other posts and finally a telephone pole stopped me abruptly. When I tried to open the driver's door it would not open and my leg was already starting to hurt me. The same leg I had already broken twice before. I ran down the street about two more blocks where my uncle Floyd and Aunt Toots were living and woke them up. My uncle went with me back to my car where I had wrecked. He helped me pick up empty beer cans from the car and took me home. The next day I called the Sheriff's department and they sent out Burt, one of the Deputy's from Leedey.

He interviewed me and gave me a ticket for reckless driving. I should have been arrested for a DUI, but back then the cops were probably too lenient with us. I probably got a ticket every week for driving in a manner not reasonable and proper and made the Vici Beacon newspaper in the legal section showing the tickets I got for that week. I think each ticket costs me $45.

After the wreck my dad felt guilty because we got in a fight over taking out the water cooler A/C out of the dining room window. I had been working on a belt that night and had planned to stay home and finish making the belt when he asked me to help him take out the A/C. As usual, I thought I knew more than him and just picked up the A/C and jerked it out by myself. Because he felt guilty for me wrecking my car, he bought me a rebuilt maroon 1973 Pontiac Grand Am. My cousin Niles had the car at his body shop and sold it to my dad for $2,500. I thought the 1970 Pontiac Lemans was fast, but this car was super-fast. It had a 400 cu. inch engine, four barrel carburetor with a 400 turbo transmission and could it fly! I estimated that it probably had a top end of about 150 mph, compared to 115 mph on the Lemans. I never let anyone pass me on the highway when I was driving that Grand Am until one day a white Pontiac Grand Prix challenged me on 8th Street road going to Woodward. We were about neck and neck flying down 8th street when he went by me. Later I heard that he had blown up his engine. That was the only time I had been beaten.

It was my Junior year in the spring of 1977 and I fell in love with a little red head that came from North Dakota. Marlyn Randolph had married a widow from North Dakota that he had cut wheat for years. She had a couple of older sons and two younger daughters who were still in school at the time so they moved to Vici the fall of 1976 or spring of 1977 with Marlyn. Marlyn's mom Stella Randolph worked at Hollands 5&10 and told me about Tami when I was in there one time. Her name was Tami Andersen and her sister's name was Leann. My Grand Am probably helped me get a date with Tami and we started dating the spring of 1977 until the summer of 1977 when Marlyn thought we might be getting too serious. She was my first girlfriend and it took me a while to get over us breaking up. I drank too much during this time and became a teenage alcoholic and would sometimes show up to class drunk. I pretty much quit caring about anything. Kenny Campbell and I would drive around drinking ourselves sober. We literally drank all night until we were sober. I got to where it would take me about 12 beers to even get a buzz and then I started drinking harder liquor like Crown Royal, Black Velvet or 101 proof Everclear in lemonade, called "Cowboy Lemonade". I went to dances every Saturday night at Arnett and would get so drunk that I even started blacking out. One night I tried leaving Arnett three times but when I got out of the street lights, the center line of the highway doubled. I would literally see two center lines and didn't know which one to follow out of town. Another time I got thrown in a snow drift after getting in a fight with some boys from Higgins, Texas and had passed out because I drank some 101 proof Everclear straight out of the bottle. Junior and Charlie Salisbury and Cliff Johnson brought me home. Cliff dropped my head when they were trying to carry me into the house and my head hit the concrete porch. I came alive and started fighting all three of them when my dad came out to see what was going on. He went out to the barn to get one of the black vacuum hoses to hit me with. The next morning I woke up with both fists swelled shut and holes in my bedroom wall made out of slats and plaster. I went into the dining room table and there was my dad with a big black eye sitting across the table. I guess I had hit him during all of the commotion.

Another time in that Grand Am, Dennis Turner and I were coming back from Arnett to Vici, which is about 23 miles, and we made it in 10 minutes – including a bathroom break. Back then I thought I was invincible. One morning dad asked me where my car was. I said I didn't know but figured it was parked out from by the barn where I normally parked it. No, instead I had ran it off the road by Leo Helmick's house and got it stuck in the bar ditch and Leo drove me home that night.

Then there was the time Joe Thomas and I were dragging Broadway of Vici one Saturday night when I decided to challenge the new cop Vici had just hired. We would go through a new cop about every 6 months back then. He was parked at the Bank of Vici when I floored my Grand Am squalling my tires in low gear for about half a block, hitting second gear and burning some more rubber before hitting high gear at about 75 mph when we went by the new cop sitting at the Bank. I hit my horn which had a distinct sound like the looney tunes road runner, BEEP! BEEP! and the chase was on. We were going over 100 mph when we got to the west edge of town. We sped all the way out to Turner's corner out west of Vici and backed up facing the south and turned out our lights. The new cop came hauling ass down the highway with his lights and sirens on when he went past us. I hit my horn again BEEP! BEEP!, and he hit his brakes and turned around. I turned my lights back on and hit the gas and started down the road we called the South Run. He turned south and started pursuing us. We lost him after a couple of miles and he turned around and went back to town. We continued on around south run which would have brought us back to Vici by the dump yard. Before, we got back to Vici, we ran off into a washout and got high centered. One of the back tires was off the ground while the other back tire was pushed up into the fender. Joe and I got out and started walking back to town, but instead of following the road we decided to cut across the country. There was a moon out that night and we could see pretty well. It was about 11:00

that night when we got stuck. We had a six pack of beer with us so we started out heading toward the flashing lights of the Co-Op Elevators. We would go into a canyon with the lights being directly to the north of us and come out of the canyon with the lights now being to the east of us. We crossed wheat fields that were waist high with the wheat headed out and wet from the rain we had just gotten and the terraces would be full of water. I stepped into one terrace that was full of water and walked out of my boots stepping into the muddy water with my socks and then had to find my boot. The beer we were carrying got heavy and we ended up tossing it rather than drinking it. It seemed like it took us forever to get to the edge of Vici and when we did we were at the south edge of the airport runway. It was about 1:30 to 2:00 am by then and we had no cell phones back then so we headed for the nearest payphone in town. The nearest payphone was outside the Dobson Telephone building on the corner of Main and Broadway. When we got there, the new cop was sitting in his car reading a newspaper. We didn't want to disturb him so we went east down the alley to the Deuce of Hearts Motel, which had the only other payphone in town. I called out to the house and my sister Willneta answered. Willneta and Kerry had just gotten married so they were staying out at the house at this time. Kerry came to town and picked me and Joe up by the Co-op scales.

After my little outrunning the cop episode, the cops started waiting for me out on highway 34 where you turned to come to our house. One night I was coming home from Woodward and instead of coming up to our turn off I took the short-cut by the curve on Highway 34 and came home. Meanwhile, the cops and mom and dad were waiting for me at the main turnoff. Another time the cop from Vici followed me home to make sure I made it and then turned on his lights when he left, I guess to let mom and dad know I was home safely. I can't imagine the worry I must have put my parents through back then. I know my dad bought a $10,000 whole life insurance policy on me probably thinking I would not make it to my 18th birthday. After I tore up the rear end in that Grand Am, my dad had Charles Campbell put a low speed rear end in it for me, before I killed myself or someone with me. After that, the Grand Am would only top out at 95 mph.

It was around June 1977 when the Grand Am saw its last days of thrill riding. My friend Joe Thomas was getting ready to go on wheat harvest that summer and he came to my house to get some 8track tapes I had borrowed. I told him that they were over at Dennis Turner's house. I had a hangover from the night before so I told Joe to drive my Grand Am. We went to Dennis's house, got the tapes and on our way back to our house a pickup went through the intersection. Joe was not a very skilled driver, or he could have missed the pickup but in-stead of hitting the brakes or trying to swerve and miss him, it's like Joe just gunned it and we T-boned the pickup right in the middle of the intersection. I was afraid that the insurance company would not pay for the collision so I changed positions with Joe and we told the other driver, Lorence Brooks that I was driving. The OHP was called out to investigate the accident and we stuck to our story that I was the driver. Long story short, the insurance paid off the claim and my cousin Niles Young, who we bought the car from, said the Grand Am was totaled. The insurance paid my dad the $2,500 for the value of the car and now my dad finally got the $2,500 I owed him for the car, except now I was without a vehicle to drive.

It didn't take me long to solve my vehicle problem. My friend Matt Ray and I saw a 1968 Oldsmobile Cutlass sitting in the car lot off of Main Street in Woodward, Oklahoma. It was forest green, two doors, with no motor, but did have a 2 speed power glide transmission in it. Matt said we should be able to take the 350 cu. in. engine out of my old Lemans that I had wrecked and hook it right up to the power glide transmission. And sure enough, I bought the Cutlass body for $100 and towed it to our farm where Matt and I went to work on rebuilding me car number 3 within about 13 months of buying car number 1. First we had to go get car number 1 from the salvage yard in Vici. I actually drove it home flying like the wind over 100 mph. When we got it home under one of the mulberry trees, we hooked a chain onto a limb and lifted the car up. The driver's front tire just fell off. If it had done that while driving home I would have totaled it again and who knows what would have happened to me. Matt was successful in taking out the old engine and installing it into the 1968 Cutlass, and in no time I had another car. I spent about $1,000 putting new mag wheels and some 50 tires on the rear end making it look like a real hot rod. I stole the Monroe air shocks off of the Grand Am that was sitting at Nile's Body shop and put on the Cutlass to jack up the rear end. I installed the CB Radio and antenna and power boost speakers and 8track tape player out of the Lemans and car number 3 was ready. We pulled the Lemans into the east tree rows and that is where it sat for over 10 years before the new owners hauled it off. The 1968 Cutlass had a top end of 130 mph and would last me until my senior year. This was the car that I backed into the gas pumps, which did not total it out but my hot rodding days were drawing to an end. I knew I had to change my ways after backing into the gas pumps and my insurance being cancelled by Farm Bureau.

Finally, my senior year had arrived and college was being talked about. Everyone was taking their ACT test to enter college and the Principal Cleo Moran told us that we could miss one day of class to go take the exam. My friend John Salisbury told me to go take the test at Panhandle A&M at Goodwell, Oklahoma and we could stay at his brother's place in Stratford,

Texas, a short distance away. I agreed and John and I went to stay with Ken Salisbury at Stratford the night before the ACT Test. We partied and drank beer the entire night and to be honest I really don't remember taking the test that next day, but I guess I did because I got my test results back in a couple of weeks. My principal Cleo Moran called me into his office and said "how in the hell do you make a 4 on an ACT test?" I had been selected for Salutatorian that year and here I only made a 4 on my college entrance test. Needless, to say I did not have going to a college as a high priority at this time in my life.

That spring I found a 1973 Chevrolet Cheyenne pickup for sale for $2,500 at a car lot in Shattuck, Oklahoma. I bought the pickup with some of my hog money. I used that pickup for hauling hog feed, hauling hay and going to and from school. I sold my old 1968 Cutlass to Matt Ray.

I had bought my class ring when I was a junior in high school and had been helping dad build fence on the Antis place when I noticed the ring was missing. I had play practice at the school that night and thought just maybe if I drove down the fence row I might find my ring that night if my lights reflected off of it. Sure enough after about 10 minutes, something shined from the headlights hitting it and I found my class ring.

During my senior year I went to school until noon and then worked the afternoon in the VAOT program. I tried many jobs including working at Wal-Mart at Woodward for about 3 weeks, driving a tractor for Bill Phillips, a farmer from Sharon, building fence for Junior Baird, another farmer from Sharon and working at the Woodward Livestock barn with my brother Charles who had moved back to Vici. I never had a steady girlfriend my Senior year and was more of a loner, looking for something to fulfill my life and make me whole. I knew I had a drinking problem that was going to ruin me if I did not do something about it. We went on our senior trip to Branson, Missouri and all we did was drink and play cards. There were a couple of us like Junior Salisbury and Randy Thompson that considered joining the Army out of high school but none of us ever did.

I graduated in May 1978 and gave my Salutatorian speech in front of the crowd sober that night. I had no idea what to do with my life, but had a few small scholarships to consider. I decided to accept the $400 scholarship from Northwestern Oklahoma State University in Alva, Oklahoma, where my brother Larry had attended 1-1/2 years before enlisting in the Army. I had another scholarship from Oklahoma State University in Stillwater but was afraid OSU was too large for a small town boy like me.

L to R: Allyson Shaw, Jan Hunter, Steve Owens, Jim Young, Mary Steinmetz,
Rickey Badley, Eddie Berry, Mark Outhier

May 1978 me wearing my Salutatorian honor cords

CHAPTER 11

Harvest of 1978

My uncle Keith McDonald had been going on wheat harvest since he was a kid with his dad. He now owned his own Combine and wheat truck and made the trip every year cutting wheat from Texas to North Dakota just short of the Canadian border. Keith was on his 2nd wife, Lynda who too had been harvesting wheat with her former husband Lynn Espy years before meeting and marrying my uncle Keith.

Keith was an easy going guy who had a drinking and gambling problem, plus he smoked. I'm not sure why my parents agreed to let me go with Keith and Lynda that summer knowing that I had a drinking problem myself but they did and I was excited to get away from the farm for one summer. My brother Charles was there to help dad and would be there while I went to college that fall.

Keith and Lynda came up from cutting wheat in Texas and southern Oklahoma about the time I graduated from High School in May 1978. I helped him by driving his old white 1970 Dodge wheat truck, hauling wheat out of the fields and into the town's grain elevators or out to a farmer's grain bins. Prior to me driving the truck, Lynda had been doing so. We cut my dad's wheat fields and some other farmers around Vici, prior to moving on to Kansas, Nebraska, South Dakota and North Dakota.

Keith had the 1970 Dodge Truck that he loaded the header off of the 105 John Deere Combine in the back. He then pulled a combine trailer holding the 105 John Deere Combine. Lynda followed behind Keith in their 1975 green and white Chevrolet Scottsdale pickup pulling a 20' travel trailer. His pickup held our diesel fuel tanks for fueling the combine and had his tool box behind the LP tank. I followed behind Lynda in my gold and white 1973 Chevrolet Cheyenne pickup and helped change tires that might blow out on the combine trailer or travel trailer. In the pickup with Lynda were their two Pomeranian dogs Cocoa and Bridget. Later on, there would be 5 as they had a litter of pups while on harvest. Keith and Lynda would sleep in the main bed of the travel trailer while I would sleep overhead in a bunk like bed. The dogs would sleep on the floor.

The state of Oklahoma had just lowered the drinking age of from 21 down to 18 the year of 1978, so I was actually of legal age to drink in Oklahoma when we left on wheat harvest. Other states still required you to be 21 to drink while yet other states required you to be 19 to drink. I loved the life of a custom harvester that summer. Beer back then costs $8.00 for a case and Marlboros cost $.55 a pack. I was smoking about 2 packs a day back then and drank my fair share of beer.

Keith had been custom harvesting over 30 years by the time I was old enough to go on harvest with him. He was the youngest of my mom's brothers and was a good man. Little kids and dogs loved him. Back in high school he was a handsome young man and all the girls wanted him. He was now approaching 50 years old, was on his second wife Lynda, had no children of his own but was still a fun uncle to be around. My brother Billy had gone on harvest with Keith in 1960, 1961 and 1962. One of my cousins Arthur McDonald had helped him cut wheat a couple of years before I went.

Keith always travelled with Marlyn Randolph on his route up to North Dakota. Maryln, his wife Doris and her two daughters Tami and Leann Andersen went on harvest with us the summer of 1978. Keith drove a 105 John Deere Combine while Marlyn always seemed to have the best equipment driving a 6600 John Deere combine with an air conditioned cab. Keith's combine had a cab too but it seemed like his air conditioner was always breaking down. Keith's wife Lynda was my best friend Matt Ray's mother-in-law. Her daughter Sandy (Espy) Ray was in Willneta's class and had graduated in 1977 with Willneta.

We cut wheat in Kansas before moving on to Nebraska where I remember cutting wheat on a large farm where the farmer was building a huge Quonset building for storing the grain. I had to auger the wheat out of the truck instead of dumping into a grain elevator like most of my previous hauls. On one of these farms the farmer had a harvest party at his barn with a dance. I remember getting pretty drunk that night and going up to the hay loft of his barn and jumping out of the hay loft to the ground below. I about rebroke my leg that I had broken twice before.

One Sunday morning we left to go to our next cutting destination and we had like three blowouts on the combine trailer that day. I remember Keith saying that it was God's way of punishing us for working on a Sunday. I think we ran out of spare tires that day and had to find a store that would open up and sell us some new tires. I can't remember which state we were in at the time.

We worked our way up through Chadron, Nebraska before going into South Dakota and going to Hot Springs, South Dakota where we stopped for the night and made camp at an RV park. Keith and Lynda took me to a spring fed swimming pool where the water was mineral water. I had never been able to swim as a kid, but all of the sudden it seemed like I could swim in this water. From Hot Springs we went further up into South Dakota to Rapid City. Rapid City had a greyhound dog race track that Keith took me to. Keith had picked the trifecta, or winners of the first three races before the race started so he was up over five hundred dollars after the third race. I had done ok myself and was up about $200. We should have quit after the 3rd race but we didn't and by the time we finished after all 12 races, we barely had enough to buy a beer. Of course while we were in Rapid City, we went to see Mt. Rushmore, which I thought was so neat.

While we were in Rapid City, South Dakota we went to a movie theatre. There was a huge entertainment bus parked outside the theatre that said Aerosmith on it. I asked Keith and Lynda who Aerosmith was. I was a country and western fan back then and didn't even realize a famous rock and roll band was sitting right behind us in the theatre. I just thought they were a bunch of long hair hippies left over from the sixties.

Keith and Lynda knew how to enjoy harvest. We worked hard during the day but then we would clean up and go into town and enjoy an evening meal. We went to Deadwood South Dakota, and went to a restaurant that looked like a Railroad Depot. We ordered before dinner drinks, wine with our meal and then after dinner drinks, like grasshoppers, or pink squirrels. We stopped and visited Deloris and Pinky Webber while we were in Rapid City, South Dakota and played cards like pitch, spades, hearts and cribbage, drinking coffee all night long. I got the worse headache from drinking too much caffeine, worse than I got from drinking beer.

I remember meeting and being passed by hundreds of motorcycles that were heading to the big motorcycle gathering in Sturgis, South Dakota. I always had a fear of motorcycle gangs from watching movies about the Hells Angels and other notorious gangs. A couple years prior to going on harvest with Uncle Keith, there had been a motorcycle gang that came to Vici and took residence at the house Keith was living. Keith and his first wife Lois had been away on harvest that year and my mom and dad were looking after their house that summer. Lois had a son named Butch who was a big guy that belonged to a motorcycle gang. He had brought that gang to our little town which frightened a lot of the folks around Vici. They raised havoc that summer until the Woodward County Sheriff's office finally came and arrested the gang and sent them on their way. I remember going over to the house with dad and finding a gun holster that must have been built for Butch himself. It must have been like a 50 inch waist and had bullets lining the holster. The gun itself had probably already been removed by the deputies. Now we were facing hundreds of motorcycles with big bikers bearing tattoos on their large arms and women riding behind them.

Marlyn had sent Doris and her two daughters to a town to get combine parts and they had not returned yet. I remember Marlyn being worried about them and he wanted me to go with him in case he ran into any trouble finding them, like I could have done anything to help him. We drove towards the town that the girls had gone and were glad to have met them coming down the highway. We turned around and went back to where we had set up camp.

Sometimes we camped at RV parks when we made camp, but other times the farmers would let us plug our travel trailer into their electric outlets and I would dig a sewer pit to run our sewer hoses.

We cut wheat at Alexander, North Dakota where Doris and her girls had a farm being ran by her older sons. Her boys had taken over the farming operation after their dad had died. I remember ordering a hamburger in North Dakota and them not using mustard on their hamburgers. Instead they used either ketchup or mayonnaise. I think it was in North Dakota that I went into a beer joint to drink beer and they asked for my ID. I had drank beer in other states like Nebraska and South Dakota where you had to be 21 to drink and now all of the sudden they were questioning me how old I was in North Dakota where you had to be 19 to drink. I had grown a beard while on harvest that summer and probably gained over 50 pounds and a beer gut from drinking so much beer that summer. We went as far as Williston, North Dakota that year, only 40 miles from the Canadian border. I was playing pool and drinking in a beer joint that did not question my age when I met up with a couple of guys in the bar. They seemed like decent guys and asked if I could give them a ride to another nearby town. I said that I would and we took off down the highway. While driving along they let me know that they were gay. I had never been confronted by anyone gay at the time and I was pretty drunk at the time. I kicked them out and left them stranded on the highway and drove off. I remember going back to the travel trailer that night and ate the last dill pickle in a pickle jar and drank all of the pickle juice from the jar.

The summer was winding down and time was coming that I had to leave Keith and Lynda and head back for College. Keith paid me $1,800 for my labor that summer and I headed back to Oklahoma following Rick and Cheryl Hanlon whom we had met on harvest. I had been following Keith and his caravan all that summer and was getting over 20 MPG with my 1973 Chevrolet pickup. When I followed Rick Hanlon back to the Colorado border, I was lucky to get 8 MPG. We drove in excess of 100 MPH most of the way and never did get a ticket. Back then it seemed like I had an intuition and could tell when a cop was nearby. Before coming back to Vici, I dropped down into Colorado and went to visit my brother Billy and his family at Evergreen, Colorado.

When I got to Billy's place, he and Joe Mac were putting up hay from the meadow. I had been hauling hay from the time I was 8 so I helped Billy and Joe Mac. Little did I know that I was out of shape from drinking beer most days plus the altitude of Colorado was taking the wind out of me, not to mention I smoked too much. Joe Mac and I took a ride into Evergreen one evening and I took a turn too fast around a ninety degree curve and hit one of the ranch fences and broke the taillight on my pickup. We had to go into Evergreen to find a new taillight. I left Billy's place and came back to Vici to get ready to go to college.

Visiting my Uncle Keith in the Nursing home prior to him passing away in 2015. My daughter Ashley, grandson Landon and great nephew Tavith in the background.

CHAPTER 12

Off to College

I had decided to take the $400 a semester scholarship offered by Northwestern State University at Alva, Oklahoma rather than the scholarship offered by OSU at Stillwater. Jim Peck and Connie Woods had also decided to go to Alva, plus there were other Vici boys and girls that were going to Alva at the time like Fred Schamburg, Lain White, Mark Farnsworth, Dianne Moss and Claretta Lingenfelter.

I was going to college to pursue being an Industrial Arts Instructor, like David Clem or Gary Adams my former shop teachers. I was paying for my room and board on a monthly basis at $110 per month. My tuition was pretty much taken care of by the scholarship I had received. Jim Peck and I were supposed to have separate rooms in Coronado Hall, the boy's dormitory of the college. We had both gone out and bought king size sheets and bedspreads for our rooms because each room had two twin size beds in them, which would make into one king size bed.

When we checked into Coronado Hall that fall we were told that we would have to share a room with one another as the enrollment was higher than expected. We were given room A of a 3 bedroom suite. Room B was being occupied by Lain White from Vici and Kenny Kauk from Leedey, and room C was being occupied by two boys from Medford and Lamont, Oklahoma, Kip Swaggard and Kris Wortz.

There wasn't supposed to be any cooking in the dorms but Jim Peck and I had a toaster oven that we used for cooking our own steaks. We decided to go ahead and push the two twin size beds together and making one king size bed rather than sleeping in the twin size beds that we did not have sheets or bedspreads for.

I had enrolled in Biology, History since the Civil War, English, Basic Electricity and Drafting that first and only semester at NWOSU, a total of 16 hours. I had never had to study in high school but was about to find out that wasn't going to work in college. All of the sudden I was responsible for getting up and getting to class on time, hustling to the next class and figuring out time management as well as developing studying habits, while partying with my friends.

Alva was a great little college town. It wasn't too big and I got to meet a lot of friends from surrounding towns in Northwestern Oklahoma. There was a pizza parlor called The Olive Pit that served the best pizza covered in mozzarella cheese that you almost had to cut with a knife. They served pitchers of beer and we drank from frosted mugs. After all Oklahoma had changed the drinking age from 21 to 18 in 1978 and we were the first college students to drink legally as freshmen.

In August 1978, Connie Woods invited Jim Peck and me to go over to Enid to visit one of our old classmates, Pam Bridges. Connie was taking a girl that she had met in the girl's dormitory on campus with her. Her name was Kathy Wolf and she was from Woodward, Oklahoma. Boys from Vici normally did not date girls from Woodward because they were known to be stuck up and didn't associate with boys from small towns like Vici, Sharon, Camargo and Leedey. We took Jim's black 1977 Chevrolet Silverado pickup, which had camper special windows and one bench seat in the cab. Back then four people could sit in the front seat of a pickup comfortably, not like today's trucks that you probably can't even get a bench seat in from the factory. We decided that we better take a little beer with us for the 60 mile journey, so we went to the Jiffy Trip on the south edge of town and bought a case of Coors and a bag of ice and put in the ice chest in the back of Jim's pickup. I think Connie was trying to match up Kathy with Jim Peck that day but instead I met my soulmate on that ride to Enid. I hadn't dated anyone since Tami Andersen when I was sixteen and hadn't shown any interest in finding someone until I met Kathy. I knew that I had a drinking problem and I was looking for someone that could straighten me out.

We weren't supposed to eat in the dorms but Jim and I had that toaster oven he brought with him and we would cook steaks and frozen fries in it. Kathy and Connie would come over and join us. My dad had picked a couple of black diamond watermelons out of our field and they went over well with the other dormitory guys.

Alva had some clubs and night spots for college students to go and party. There was the Nite Lite, Gina's and the Twig. The Nite Lite was more of a dance place that served drinks and played disco music which was very much the craze at this time. Gina's was a bar next to the Olive Pit that college students hung out and the Twig was more of a gentlemen's club strip bar north of the Nite Lite. The Knotty Pine was a local beer joint more down town that was painted pink, where locals came to drink beer. I frequented all four at different times while living in Alva. In addition, the college itself would sponsor some mixers to get students to know one another. Kathy and I went to one of the mixers shortly after meeting then we started going to the Nite Lite and Gina's when we went out.

Jim Peck and I would make pitchers of Cowboy Lemonade and Purple Passion using lemonade and grape juice and 101 Everclear and take to the dances or just drive around Alva drinking. One morning we came out after one of our partying binges and tried to find my pickup. Kathy and Connie had hid it in another parking lot. Another time we found my pickup parked next to the Coronado Hall so close that both the front and back bumpers were touching the north brick wall of Coronado Hall. It took me quite a while to get the pickup away from the wall without scratching the wall itself. Then there was the time that I took Fred Schamburg on a ride out south of town around a wheat field that never had a fence around it. Instead the wheat field had telephone poles on the north side of it next to the road. I took Fred on a little ride around the poles going about 60 mph scaring the crap out of him.

We used to speed going home and coming back to college. Mark Farnsworth lived in Sharon, Oklahoma and sometimes he and I would run front door for one another on the drive back to college or sometimes it might be Lain White or Kenny Kauk that would run the front or back door for me. One night Mark was running the front door telling me where his 10-20 was and saying that no bears were in sight. I listened to his advice when all of the sudden an Oklahoma Highway Patrol came out of nowhere and turned his lights on me. His name was Crabtree and this would be my first time I had ever been pulled over for a speeding ticket, believe it or not. My intuition had failed me for once and this same OHP officer would get me again later for a second speeding ticket over around Kiowa, Kansas before going into Kansas.

As time went by and I partied too much, that $1,800 I earned on wheat harvest wasn't going to last me much longer. The $110 per month for room and board and all the beer, cigarettes and gas money I used had pretty much drained my checking account. I decided that maybe I should drop out of college and get a job. I knew my brother Larry was doing good in the oil patch working on drilling rigs but I didn't want to leave Alva or Kathy whom I had fell in love with by now. It was now October 1978 and I had to make the tough choice of what to do to survive. My dad had told me that the banker at Vici would probably give me a loan to go to college, but I didn't want to go into debt for college. Instead I decided to quit college after 10 weeks and find a job and then maybe start back in the spring if I had enough money. I remember going to talk with Dean of the college about withdrawing from College. He tried to talk me out of it but I would not listen to him. I'll never forget the reception I got from my dad when I told him that I had quit college. The look on his face told it all. He told me that I probably wasn't smart enough to make it through college anyway. Maybe he was right after all. I hadn't been too smart in handling money or time while in college. My favorite subject had been History and I was making a C or D in it, plus the Basic Electricity class was eating my lunch and I had already dropped it before quitting college all together. I was making a B in English, and an A in Biology and a B in Drafting, which I really liked.

CHAPTER 13

Back on the Farm

I can't remember the exact date, but one day in October 1978 I went into the Knotty Pine and asked the bar owner if he knew of anyone needing help. He told me about a large corporate farmer from Burlington, Oklahoma that owned a huge farm. His name was Ross Kasparek. He said that Ross normally came into the beer joint on a normal basis and might be coming by later that day. I kind of hung around the bar until he showed up and introduced myself to him. He was about 45, medium height, and had a mustache wearing a cowboy hat. I told him that I was looking for work and he asked me if I could weld. I told him yes that welding was one of my favorite things to do. He told me that he and his wife Glenda raised registered mini Dobermans and Whippets and that he needed some welding done on his kennel pens. We negotiated terms of temporary employment and then the next day I showed up to his farm to start welding ramps for a dog kennel. I met his wife Glenda, his hired hands Mark and Jose, and his father Paul. He showed me a Lincoln gasoline operated welder that I would use for building the ramps in the shop and then later install in the kennel.

When I first went to work for Ross, I was still living in the dormitory. After a couple days of working for Ross, he took a liking to me and asked if I would consider working for him permanently as a farm hand. He had found out that I had lived on a farm all my life and he gave me an offer of $800 a month, a farm house to live in and a company pickup to drive. I accepted his offer just in time to move out of Coronado Hall and move to the Jones farm house just southwest of Burlington.

Kasparek Farm, Inc. as it was called was the name of Ross's corporation farm consisting of several thousand acres of wheat farms made up of small farms he had purchased over the years. I just happened to live on the Jones' farm that he had purchased a couple years before coming to work for him. He told me that if I worked six months for him that I would earn half of a beef. The house I lived in was a three bedroom house with a dining room, bath room, living room and kitchen. On the east side of the house was a chicken house full of egg laying hens that I was responsible for feeding and gathering eggs each day. On the north side were over 1,000 head of hogs on feeders that were being taken care of by another hand named Kevin. Kevin handled all of Ross's hog operations and did not live in one of Ross's farm houses like me, Jose or Mark. On the south side of my house was a barn with corrals used for cattle or sheep. When I first moved in the corral was empty, but later we would work cattle over there and then later Ross would move several hundred head of sheep through it.

Over at Ross's farm house was the main operation where he ran over 3,000 head of feeder sheep under covered sheds that housed huge feeders that we ground sheep feed almost every day. Back west of Ross's house was where Jose and Mark lived in a trailer house and a pen full of 900 head of Ewes that were lambing. And back behind Jose and Mark's trailer there was a dead pit where dead steers, pigs, and sheep were dumped if they died. Several miles east of there were the wheat fields where another 1,500 head of sheep were grazing on winter wheat. North of Ross's farm house were some more wheat pastures where he had four or five hundred head of steers grazing on wheat pasture and another four or five hundred head of steers on a pasture just south of Ross's place. Then he had a Guernsey cow we called Abigail that he had me milk each morning and night that lived on the wheat field east of the barn along with a couple of quarter horses. One of the quarter horses was name Bud and he was about a 15 hand horse with a wide back. I rode him almost every day bareback to bring in Abigail for her twice a day milking. The Kennels were just south of Ross and Glenda's house as was the hay shed where we stored the alfalfa round hay bales for sheep feed. A large tub grinder sat next to the hay shed used for grinding the hay up for mixing with grain and minerals for the sheep feed. The machine shed was north east of Ross's house and the barn was northwest of Ross's house. In addition to the dogs, Glenda raised for selling, they had two full size Dobermans named Joe and Rojo. Joe was a black and tan Doberman while Rojo was a red Doberman. Then Glenda had a little Whippet dog that would always bite my ankles when I would walk from the machine shed out to the kennels. I hated that little dog, but don't remember his name.

One Sunday, Belinda brought mom and dad out to the farm at Burlington to visit me. It was my Sunday to work that weekend and I was out by the kennels when they drove up in the drive. Ross and Glenda were away that weekend so they had let Joe out of the kennel to guard the farm house. Belinda opened the door on the car and mom was getting out when Joe noticed them in the drive and went charging towards them barking very loudly. I hollered "JOE" at the top of my lungs and just like that he sat down and quit pursuing them. It about scared my mom to death. I didn't realize that I could actually control Joe. He was used to me working on the kennels and he had one of the pens in the kennel where he chewed on empty Coors cans for entertainment.

We worked six days a week from sun up to sun down which equated to about 11 hours a day during the October 1978 – January 1979. We got every other Sunday off so no one had to work every Sunday. I got a blue 1976 four wheel drive Chevrolet pickup to drive with a Motorola radio in it to communicate with Ross, Jose or Mark. We also had another Mexican working for us when I started to work named Ben. He had just run the 2030 John Deere tractor out of oil and burned up the engine. I think it was because of this that I got the job working for Ross. The tractor had been taken to the John Deere Shop in Alva to rebuild the engine. It was the tractor used for lifting the round hay bales and putting them into the tub grinder. With the 2030 John Deere tractor out of commission, Ross had us using an old U.S. Army backhoe and its bucket for putting the bales into the grinder.

Ross was a wheeler dealer and in addition to running a huge corporate farm he was a dealer for livestock pesticide dust bags used for keeping flies off of cattle. And then there was the constant deliveries of heavy equipment and machinery that came to the farm and luxury conversion vans. One morning I would show up to work and there would be a U.S. Army backhoe setting on a low boy trailer or a U.S. Air Force front end loader or maybe an Army bulldozer. Glenda would get a new customized Van with a refrigerator in it or a new Cadillac Eldorado to drive about twice a month. I never once questioned what was going on because I just saw Ross as quite the entrepreneur. One day I observed Mark Clark, one of the ranch hands, using a grinder on the U.S. Air Force front end loader. I asked him what he was doing. He just answered me, "Oh, I'm just grinding the serial numbers off," and laughed. I never gave it another thought.

Mark Clark I found out was an ex-felon working on the farm and he was dating the farmer's daughter or at least Glenda's daughter, Karen. Karen was a senior in high school. Mark liked to drink peppermint schnapps out of a little flask shaped bottle he carried in his coat. He would give me a shot every once in a while to keep me warm on some of those cold winter days we endured. Jose Flores was an older Mexican hand that I figured was about 30 years old while Mark I believe was 26. Jose and I used to ride horses out on the wheat fields looking for steers that were showing signs of being sick. Jose was a pretty good roper and I loved to run my horse alongside steers and wrestle them to the ground like a bulldogger. One day we were doctoring the cattle when Jose roped one and got his index finger caught between the rope and the saddle horn. He broke his finger so Glenda had to tape it up for him. Another day Mark and I were looking over some sheep in the wheat field when we saw a coyote running west of the sheep. I happened to have my 30-30 in the truck so I took a bead on the coyote and led him a few feet before pulling the trigger. The coyote went rolling and then fell limp. We drove up to it and took it back to my house to sell the hide.

I loved working on the corporate farm and working with both Mark and Jose. A typical day of working usually consisted of getting up in the morning, feeding the chickens at my house and then driving over to Ross and Glenda's house. I would then go get on Bud the quarter horse and retrieve Albatross Abigail out of the north wheat field, milk her and take the milk to Glenda. We would then go to the east wheat fields and check the sheep and make sure they had water in the tanks and break any ice if need be. Then we would go take some round hay bales using Mark's truck that had a round hay bale fork on the back and deliver the hay to steers in the north wheat fields, break the ice on their tanks and make sure there were no sick or dead steers to retrieve and take to the dead pit. Then we would start our daily routine of grinding alfalfa hay bales in the huge tub grinder and make feed for the sheep under the covered sheds. My day ended by milking the cow again and gathering eggs at my house. We had a few jobs that took us away from the farm like picking up more alfalfa hay bales on trucks and one time we went to Lamont to get some more pig feeders for Kevin who ran the hog operation, but pretty much our daily routine involved grinding sheep feed.

It was probably in early December that Ross told Mark and I that he had bought some Texas sheep that he wanted us to vaccinate in the corrals of my farm place. Mark and I were instructed to vaccinate them with four different vaccines or shots and to mark each of the sheep with a different colored chalk to designate which vaccine we used. We had a blue, red, pink and yellow marker to use for each shot. We were moving right along vaccinating the sheep when Mark thought it would be funny to paint the sheep with some more decorative markings than a stripe across the back. Before long we were giving the sheep rings around their eyes and then around their butt holes that looked like we were painting targets on them. We were amused at our own work until Ross showed up with a prospective buyer of the sheep. Boy did we get an ass chewing from Ross for our creative endeavors.

Kathy had pretty much moved into the farm house with me, after I started working at Ross's. She even helped me vaccinate new feeder pigs that had arrived over at Ross's house, prior to moving to the pens north of my house. We had fun chasing and catching them in the mud until each had been vaccinated. One day I let her shoot all of my guns that I had brought out to the farm. I let her shoot my .22lr first which had no kick, then my 12 gauge. Shotgun which had a little more kick. Then I let her shoot my 30-30 rifle which she thought would kick like the .22lr but instead it about knocked her shoulder off and she threw the gun to the ground. I'm sure my laughing about it did not help the matter, and she said that she would never shoot guns with me again.

I shot my first male pheasant in the hog pen behind the house I lived and put his breast in the freezer to eat. I never did get to eat that pheasant. I remember going to gather eggs in the hen house one night after it was already dark. I felt in each hen's nest for eggs when all of the sudden I saw two red eyes looking at me on top of one of the roosts. It was a large owl which had been raiding the hen house. It flew out of the house and about scared me to death and I never gathered eggs after dark again.

Since I had a company pickup to drive I let Kathy drive my pickup back and forth to college. One day she went around the circle drive in front of my house and turned too short and caught the guide line cable securing a light pole in the yard. The cable went under the cab of the truck and then came up and caught the bed of the truck ripping it back to the back wheel. I came out of the house just as she did it. She thought I was going to shout at her but I just blew it off as an accident. I couldn't get mad at her if I tried. I had finally found my soulmate and wasn't going to do anything to screw it up. I had remembered Charles and Nina and how they used to fight and that was one lesson I learned as a kid that I was not going to repeat. A few weeks later we were in Alva where I opened up a checking account at Central National Bank in November of 1978. An old man ran the stop light and hit the side that Kathy had torn back on my pickup. His insurance ended up paying for replacing the entire side.

Kathy and I laughed about the kitchen counter top that had a steel ring around it. Every time you would open the refrigerator door and touch the counter top at the same time it would shock you. But we were so happy those couple of months. The Christmas of 1978, Kathy and I went back to celebrate with my mom and dad and we announced that we were engaged and going to be married December 12, 1979. December 12 was my mom and dad's anniversary date and that was the reason we had chosen it. I had sold a couple of calves that I still owned on the farm and had bought Kathy an engagement ring for $456. Everybody congratulated us and I think everyone approved of my choice for a wife.

During those months I was so exhausted after working 11 hours a day I could hardly stay awake when Kathy and I would go the Nite Lite to go dancing. One night when Kathy had gone home to see her parents who had moved to Buffalo, I went with Mark Clark into Alva to go partying. We went to the Twig and got kicked out of there and then we went to the Knotty Pine before going back to the farm. This was Thursday January 4, 1979 two day before my life would change forever.

CHAPTER 14

The Day My Life Changed

It had been a cold start for 1979 with the temperatures being in the teens and even single digits that cold January. We had done our morning duties of milking the cow, breaking ice on water tanks and feeding the steers in the north field. We were getting our equipment started up for the daily grinding of sheep feed on that cold January 6, 1979 day. It had snowed the day before and the wheat fields were covered with wet white snow. We had gotten back the little 2030 John Deere tractor from PK Equipment in Alva but no one had remembered to put the spear attachment back on the GB 800 Front End Loader. We had been using a John Deere backhoe bucket to load the round hay bales into the tub grinder. We now had our favorite tractor back used for lifting and dumping the hay bales into the grinder without having to use a rope to secure the bales to the backhoe bucket. Mark had started up the 4630 John Deere tractor used for running the tub grinder and engaged the PTO that spun the grinder's knife blades and I had just raised the first alfalfa hay bale and let it drop into the grinder, using the 2030 John Deere tractor.

Mark was in the Chevy feed truck where the hay was being shot into off of the conveying belt of the grinder. I had just slid the pallet attachments of the front-end loader under the second hay bale of the day and backed up with the bale straight in front of me on the front-end loader. I looked over to Mark to make sure the feed truck was still running on such a cold morning to make sure the hay did not pile up. If the truck had died, then the auger in the truck bed would not circulate the loose hay and would enable it to pile up and overflow over the sides. Mark was sitting in the truck and gave me a thumbs up that everything was OK. I looked back to the hay bale that was supposed be in front of me, but it was not there. I looked up just as the hay bale come falling off of the front-end loader and I ducked out of reflex, but there was nowhere to go as the bale fell and hit me in the back of my shoulders and back. I had my left foot on the clutch and my right foot on the brakes when the bale hit me. The tractor was in reverse and when the impact of the bale hit me, the bale also hit the right fender of the tractor and crushed it into the right rear tire. Because the tractor was in reverse and because my feet instantly came off of the clutch and brakes, the tractor started spinning and cutting donuts in reverse. Mark saw what happened and jumped from the truck to come to my aid.

Mark chased the tractor around in circles until he finally reached the kill switch on the tractor and shut it down. I was sitting in the seat wobbling like a bowl of Jell-O. The impact had instantly paralyzed me from the chest down and I had no balance sitting in the seat. Mark immediately raised Ross by using the Motorola Radio in my pickup. Within minutes Ross was on the scene and asking me what he could do. I told him to just knock me out, that the pain was more than I could bear. Instead he and Mark lifted me off of the tractor and put me in the back of the pickup and put their coats over me and waited for the ambulance to arrive. Ross told me that he wanted to help me so bad but just couldn't knock me out like I wanted him to.

The ambulance came and they put me on a back board and loaded me into the ambulance and transported me to Kiowa, Kansas where they took me to the Emergency Room. The doctor there said that the injury was too serious for them to treat and recommended that I be transported to Wesley Medical Center in Wichita, Kansas. They had discussed taking me to Oklahoma City at first but Wichita was closer and the roads were in better shape in Kansas than Oklahoma after the snow and ice we had just had the day before. I kept pleading for them to give me some type of pain killer but they just replied that they needed me to be fully conscious and able to tell the doctors where I had pain.

The ride to Wichita seemed like an eternity to me with the worse pain I had ever felt. My broken legs and ankle seemed like nothing compared to this pain. I thought I had broken my hips from the round hay bale falling on me. I finally arrived at Wesley Medical Center where they immediately x-rayed me confirming what they had expected at Kiowa, Kansas, that my back was broken at the T-6& 7 level and that my spinal cord was bruised but not severed. They said I had a large hematoma at the point of impact and that the swelling needed to subside before they could tell if there was permanent damage. I had no feeling in my legs and feet and could not move anything below the waist or actually at mid chest level.

They said that my parents and Kathy had been notified and were on their way to see me. I told them that I did not want Kathy to see me like I was. Kathy's mom and dad took Kathy to the junction of Highway 64 out of Alva and Highway 34 out of Woodward where they met Charles, Connie, Belinda and Mom in mom's 1974 Caprice. They then took Kathy on to Kiowa, Kansas and then on to Wichita, Kansas when they found out I had been transferred there.

The orthopedic surgeon assigned to my case was Forney W. Fleming, MD and the neurosurgeon was Paul S. Stein, MD.

I knew nothing about either one of them, just that I needed relief from my pain. They decided that they needed to do surgery to stabilize my spine. Dr. Fleming performed the surgery of removing a piece off of my left hip bone and fusing it to the T-6 & 7 vertebrae bones and inserting two 8" Harrington rods, one on each side to stabilize the fused bones. I assume that Dr. Stein observed or assisted during the surgery.

It wasn't long after the surgery that Dr. Stein delivered the bad news to me that I would never walk again and that I would probably never be able to have children. I remember looking at my mom and Kathy after receiving that news and telling Kathy that she needed to leave me and go on with her life, but she refused and stuck with me instead. She hung a picture in my room of a mouse pushing an elephant up a hill with the caption below it saying "Where there is a will there is a way."

CHAPTER 15

Life at Wesley Medical

I had been in the hospital when I was 4 years old after our car accident, but don't really remember it that much. I was now lying in an Intensive Care Unit after undergoing surgery and now they said I had a blood clot in my lung and might die. I was thinking, just let it happen for I had nothing to live for. All my hopes and dreams of a life with Kathy were gone even though she refused to just let me go. I thought about what the doctor said about not being able to have children and my mind raced back to the fall of 1978 when Kathy and I went to Tulsa. We had sex for the first time that night and even though I had protection, Kathy missed her period and we were afraid that she might be pregnant. Now we were facing the possibility that children were out of the question, let alone that I would ever walk again and do the things that I had done as an active teenager.

I was taken to Wesley Medical Center in Wichita, Kansas not only because it was closer than Oklahoma City but also because it was a well-known trauma center that treated cranial and spinal injuries. The sixth floor was totally dedicated to brain and spinal patients. I met several patients on that floor that I remember today. My first roommate was Kris Jackson. Kris and his twin brother Kraig had been in a car accident and had hit some horses on a dirt road one night. Both broke their necks but Kris's brother Kraig recovered from his injuries and was not left paralyzed like Kris from the neck down. Kris was 16 years old and was a big Kiss Fan and had Kiss posters hanging all over his side of the room. My side just had the picture of the mouse pushing the elephant up the hill. Fortunately for Kris, his neck injury healed and he regained his ability to walk after breaking his neck. He had to wear a halo brace on his head and shoulders that weighed like a ton, but he walked out of that hospital. I think Kris's fracture was like a C-6 or C-7 break. He had definitely defied the odds and should have considered himself so lucky. I am sad however to report that I found Kris on the "Find a Grave" app at the time of writing this book and he died in 2016 at the age of 52. No details of how he died were attached to his memorial.

Then there was Marty Hochman who was 8 years older than me. He was from Ellsworth, Kansas and had been involved in yet another car accident while driving a friend's Corvette. The car had spun around after wrecking and hit a telephone pole. Marty was not paralyzed instantly like me but later became paralyzed when they transported him to the hospital and did not stabilize his neck with a neck brace. His break was a C-8 fracture and he had very limited use of his arms and hands. Marty was quite the comedian and made everyone laugh that he came in contact with. Once Marty got to go home, he never did gain his independence but instead his mother did a lot for him. He never did learn to drive with any type of hand controls so he never experienced that freedom. I stayed in touch with Marty over the years and encouraged him to get a set of hand controls installed but he refused to do so. Marty died in June of 1994 from septic shock after letting a urinary tract infection (UTI) go too long without treatment. Somehow, I think Marty probably knew that he was sick but was just tired of living. I've known those same feelings over the past 40 years. Nonetheless, I was notified by Marty's brother when he passed away because Marty had told Myron to contact me when he died. I found Marty's home town and visited his brother and father in 2004 when making a business trip to Denver. I considered Marty my closest friend at Wesley Medical Center.

There was a young man a few months younger than I, named Frank Evans who was on the sixth floor when I arrived on the unit. Frank was a farm boy like me who spent his entire life on a farm up at Braman, Oklahoma. He wrecked his new 1977 Ford pickup he had just purchased a month before after a homecoming party. The accident broke Frank's neck at the C-5, C-6 level making him a quadriplegic from the shoulders down. Frank said he had been drinking that night and when he woke up the first thing he saw was ceiling tiles and he knew he wasn't home. Frank still lives in Braman with his mother and still has some cattle that he pays young men around town to help take care of them. He has had bladder cancer and for the past year been bed ridden with two pressure sores they can't get to heal. I just spoke to him at the time of writing this book and he told me that a month ago, he was diagnosed with colon cancer. He had surgery August 8, 2019 to have his entire colon removed and have a colostomy bag installed. I think Frank and I are the only two original patients still living from the unit. Frank always has a good attitude when I talk to him despite his circumstances, which seem dim to me.

The worse conditioned patient on the floor was David. I can't remember his last name but David was about my age and had been injured diving into the shallow end of a swimming pool. He broke his C-1 vertebrae which impacted not only his arms and legs but also his breathing. He had to be on a ventilator just to breath. He was by far in worse condition than any of the other quadriplegics or us paraplegics. I don't know what happened to David, but I'm sure he probably did not last long given the condition he was in.

Then there was Bob Holgerson. He had been injured while on wheat harvest and had a head injury. I heard from him some years later but have no idea if he is still alive or not.

Another head injury on our floor was Butch, a motorcycle gang member who had crashed his motorcycle. All of the nurses were afraid of Butch and they had him in Gerry chair that he pushed himself around with his feet. He came to the cranial Spinal unit shortly before I was dismissed.

Jim Main was an older farmer from Caldwell, Kansas, who suffered the same accident I had. His accident happened on Dec 11, 1978 and ironically, he was driving a 3010 John Deere tractor with a GB 800 Front End Loader just like the one I had been operating at the time of my accident. He reminded me of my Uncle Check who died in 1973. His facial features were similar to Uncle Check and he was a skinny man like Uncle Check. In addition, he had the same model of tractor as my uncle. Jim was 56 years old and had his accident loading round hay bales onto a trailer. His fracture was at the T-9, T-10 level making him a paraplegic like myself. Jim and I became roommates after Kris was dismissed from the hospital. Jim's wife Joanne became good friends with Kathy and we kept in touch with her for years after Jim passed away a short 10 months after his accident. Jim died from legionnaire's disease on September 22, 1979.

While in the hospital Jim Main, Marty Hochman, Kris Jackson, Frank Evans and I became quite the crew and I became the leader. We hid from the social worker on the days we were supposed to a have our weekly social group meeting. One time we went out to the parking lot garage and went up to the rooftop level where we raced our wheelchairs down the steep grade. Kris was walking with his heavy halo brace on his head pushing Marty Hochman's wheelchair. He was zigging and zagging Marty in his chair sometimes taking a turn on two tires instead of all four, when one of the hard insert rubber tires popped off of Marty's chair. Kris and Jim had to pop the hard insert tire back on the rim while I lifted up one side of the chair with Marty still in the chair. We laughed all the way back to the sixth floor. Then there was another week that we avoided the social meeting by hiding in the janitor's closet until Cheryl, our head nurse found us and cussed us out. After that we decided maybe a better place to hide might be the morgue in the basement of the hospital. We were discovered after a short search by Cheryl and taken to our social meeting. I think the social worker thought we didn't like her but instead, we were just dealing with our situations the best way we knew how. The social worker had given me a psych test that showed I was depressed so they prescribed me valium and lithium for depression. I remembered lying in bed and feeling like the entire building was moving back and forth. Turns out it was the bed and floatation mattress that was supposed to keep me from getting pressure sores. Another time I had fathom pains in my legs and thought my legs were lying in hog troughs filled with water. Another time I remember talking to Kathy on the phone and she asked me how I was doing. I told her that I was sitting on the John Deere tractor out by the hay barn at Ross's. She said, "Let me talk to the Nurse". I gave the phone to the nurse and the nurse assured Kathy it was just the valium causing me to hallucinate. Yet another time I thought Kathy was on the outside of the Wesley Medical Center building climbing the walls. They finally quit prescribing the valium to me because of the adverse side effects.

While in Wesley Medical Center we underwent both Physical and Occupational therapy sessions. Physical Therapy helped us with range of motion of our limbs and even standing up between parallel bars to teach us how to do the swing through gate using our arms. It was tough work after having laid in bed for weeks and the muscles in my arms had weakened. When I first got injured, I probably weighed 180 pounds but now I had lost down to 135 pounds. I had weighed 155 pounds when I was 16 years old, so this was the skinniest I had been in some years. They fitted me with what they called a turtle shell brace for my back. It was basically two pieces made from a foam substance material that had Velcro straps to cinch it together. It fit fine when I weighed 135 lbs. but as I gained back the weight I lost, there became more and more space between the two pieces of the brace. The occupational therapy was meant to teach us how to take care of ourselves, like getting dressed in bed or learning how to do daily activities like cooking or transferring from our chair to bed or chair to car, or chair to toilet, etc.

While in the hospital they took us on field trips to different events. One such event was a Harlem Globetrotter's game at Wichita State University and then once we went to a rodeo at the fairgrounds. Marty was almost as entertaining as some of the events we went to.

I never had many visitors while in the hospital, but I could always count on Kathy every weekend. She would make that drive from Alva, Oklahoma to Wichita, Kansas in her 1965 Volkswagen bug. She told me that the first couple trips were pretty scary with the bad weather and that she ran off the road one time to be saved by a farmer. After that she said that farmers along the route began to look for her on Friday afternoons going to Wichita and Sunday afternoons coming back to Alva. The farmer who pulled her back onto the road the first time asked her who she was and where she was going. She answered him that her name was Kathy Wolf and that her fiancé had been injured in a farm accident on a farm in Burlington. He replied that he had heard about the accident and that from now on he would be watching for her. She worked at the Alva Livestock Sales Barn on Mondays in the café as a waitress. She would deliver coffee and pie to some of the patrons at the sale barn and one of them said, "Now tip her good she has to drive to Wichita to see her fiancé." God always seemed to open a way for her safe travels to Wichita and provide her with the money for gas to get there. In addition, to working at the sales barn, Kathy worked week day evenings at the Knotty Pine where I had gotten the job offer from Ross. Don Barr who ran the Knotty Pine felt bad about me getting hurt and always gave generously to Kathy when paying her, plus she made good tips from patrons who knew her story. Kathy stayed in the waiting room of the hospital and ate lots of toast with roast beef and gravy on top, or SOS. One time however, one of my nurses named Phyllis let her stay at her apartment and another time she stayed at my first cousin Lois Pickett's house with her and her husband, Lawrence. At that time, Wichita, Kansas was not a safe place to be with the BTK Killer on the loose. Even the hospital waiting rooms could have been just as dangerous with the killer on the loose.

After a couple of months, the hospital allowed me to take weekend leaves from the hospital. Most of the times Kathy came to get me and take me home and then bring me back to the hospital. One time, the brother of a cousin by marriage named Mike Isbell volunteered to take me home and bring me back to the hospital. Mike lived in Wichita and worked at the newspaper printing factory. His sister Rose was married to my first cousin Leon Bowman. In the early 1960s he too had lived in Vici and knew my older brothers Billy, Charles and Larry so he was excited to take me back to Vici for the weekend. Going back to Wesley Medical Center on that Sunday Mike decided that we needed take a detour before going straight back to the hospital. Instead we went to the factory where he worked. He bought me some beer and he got high smoking some weed. He offered me a smoke but I refused, but I did not refuse the beer and proceeded to get drunk. This was the first time I had anything to drink since getting hurt and my tolerance for beer had decreased and in no time, I was drunk. Mike took me back to the hospital at about midnight. I was supposed to be back by 9:00 pm. I got a big chewing out by the head nurse Cheryl who just happened to be on duty.

On March 30, 1979 after 83 days I was finally released from Wesley Medical Center to go back home. It was my Uncle Keith's 50th birthday and he brought mom and dad to the hospital in their 1974 Caprice car to bring me back home. I was excited but yet apprehensive to leave the hospital. How would I make a living and go on with life in a wheelchair?

CHAPTER 16

Going Back Home

D ad had found a couple of 2"x12" boards to use as ramps to get me onto the front porch of our house. That was the first of many barriers I had to overcome to get around in my wheelchair. The doorways of our house were wide enough to get through except for the bathroom. I had to use wash clothes to clean myself and mom was waiting on me like a nurse those couple of months that I lived at the farm house. She tried to do everything for me instead of making me do things myself. This is not what they had taught us in occupational therapy, so I tried to become more independent and with Kathy around I never had that problem because she was stern and would make me do things for myself.

My dad never seemed old to me as a kid growing up, even though he was, but now something had changed. My accident had hurt him almost as much as it did me. He couldn't believe that my life was now to be spent confined to a wheelchair.

Kathy was finishing up her spring 1979 semester at NWOSU and driving from Alva to Vici to see me instead of Alva to Wichita. Mom and dad were even letting her sleep in bed with me, which I thought strange at the time but maybe they thought that was encouraging me to get better. We found a physical therapist named Randall Martin from the Shattuck hospital who visited different nursing homes to give me treatments. One day I would meet him at the Vici Nursing Home and then maybe another day at the Mooreland Nursing Home or the Woodward Colonial Manner nursing home. He was a very patient physical therapist and thought that he could get me walking using a walker or loftstrand crutches. I worked hard trying to prove him right but the damage to my spine did not improve. At first, I thought maybe I was gaining back some movement in my left leg when I could actually make one toe move, but that was the extent of it. The left leg could not feel anything. In the other leg I could feel hot or cold water but no movement.

Kathy drove me where ever I needed to go because I did not have any hand controls installed yet. On May 14, 1979 I had to go back to Wesley Medical Center again for them to evaluate whether or not I was progressing along with my recovery as far as occupational and physical therapy was concerned. I stayed a week on the sixth floor and passed with flying colors because I could transfer from my chair to vehicle or chair to bed and toilet without help and could dress myself. Kathy took me back to Vici.

Kathy stayed out at our farm house at Vici during June 1979 and would catch a ride with a lady from Buffalo Oklahoma to go to summer school at NWOSU that month. Her name was Betty Selman and was an older well to do lady that Kathy got to know at college, who volunteered to give Kathy rides to Alva several days a week.

Sometime in June of 1979, we heard that a state-wide heavy equipment smuggling ring had been busted by the OSBI. There were several parties involved. One living in Chester, Oklahoma, one living in Quinlan, Oklahoma and one living in Burlington, Oklahoma. The one living in Burlington, Oklahoma was Ross Kasparek. Had I not been injured in January, I might very well have been arrested with Ross, his dad Paul and Mark Clark, the hired hand I worked with. Though I did not participate in any of the smuggling itself, I might have been an accessory to the crime just by association. Maybe God had removed me from that danger, but what a price I had to pay.

CHAPTER 17

My Need for Independence

In September 1973 my dad's younger brother Chelcie had died and in May 1977 his oldest brother Herbert had died. Now in July 1979, dad's second oldest brother Fred who lived in Missouri was not doing well, so he wanted to go see him before he died. Dad and mom decided to take a trip to see my Uncle Fred and they left Kathy to stay with me while they were gone. Kathy had been looking in Alva for places to rent and she told me that she had found a one bedroom garage apartment that would be perfect for us. It rented for $150 a month plus utilities. While my parents were gone Kathy moved me to Alva which gave me my independence from my mom trying to take care of me. It was the best thing that could have happened and probably prolonged my mom's life.

Our first apartment that we rented in Alva was a converted garage apartment consisting of one bedroom, one bath, a living room and a kitchen dining area. It was perfect because the bathroom door was wide enough for my wheelchair. Del Weese was our landlord; he and his wife lived next door in the house. I believe our address was 1014 ½ Fifth Street, Alva Oklahoma 73717.

Daddy said that I needed to see if there was a way to get a settlement for my damages from Ross's insurance company, so he had hired an attorney from Woodward. Ivan Duke Halley was his name and he was from Sharon, Oklahoma, a small town just north of Vici and south of Woodward. Duke had come out to our farm house and discussed my options. He first applied me for SS Disability benefits but they denied me saying that I did not have enough work experience to be eligible for disability benefits. Social Security did, however, say that I was eligible for Supplemental Security Income or SSI payments in the amount of $150 per month; the exact same amount of our rent in Alva. He then sued Ross's insurance company under his liability insurance and we received $75,000 plus medical from them. The medical costs at this point in time were a little over $26,000 for three months in a hospital plus the ambulance transportation fee and the costs of my wheelchair. Wow, you could run up that much money for one day in an ICU today. Duke's fee was one quarter of what I received if we did not go to court or 1/3 if we did. With the money from Ross's insurance company we paid off all of the medical bills and Duke's fee. We then went to Brown's Ford over at Shattuck, Oklahoma to look at new Ford Thunderbirds and found one that we liked. The salesman acted like we didn't have any money to buy anything from him so we went to Woodward to the Ford dealer and found the exact same 1979 Ford Thunderbird which we bought for $7,900. The car salesman was Woodward's football coach Jim Phillips. We wrote a check for the car and then went furniture shopping for my mom and dad at Goin's Furniture in Woodward. We bought them a sleeper sofa and chair for the living room and a new recliner for my dad. After getting mom and dad's living room set we bought us a new Charles Schneider sleeper sofa, a new 19" Magnavox TV and Magnavox Odyssey game system with multiple game cartridges. We also bought a new 15 cu. inch Kenmore chest freezer at Sears in Alva and a filing cabinet with a safe in it. The rest of the money we put in my savings account at Alva.

After we got our initial settlement from Ross's Insurance Company Social Security notified us that we needed to pay them back the $150 a month of SSI payments. We had only received 3 of them at the time. We argued with them and told them that the payments were used to cover our rent and other than that we had completely exhausted my savings prior to the settlement. They didn't care one way or the other and I remember the young lady that was demanding us to pay back the money was in a wheelchair herself. I think I stuck to my guns and never did pay them back.

Kathy and I were happy to be on our own living in that one bedroom apartment. One day Kathy found two little kittens next to the apartment that she brought in to feed. They were wild and scared. One was a yellow tabby like Morris the cat, so we called him Morris. The other one was a light yellow with white markings and looked more like a cougar, so we called him Charlie. They became our first pets and rode in the back window of our Thunderbird like a couple of cherubs guarding our back seat. They would sit in the back window of the T-Bird and hiss at birds that landed near our car when we went to the Sonic in Alva. We took them with us everywhere including to mom and dad's farm. Once when we went to the farm Charlie caught like 10 mice in a matter of several minutes from our separator room. He would catch one and drop it at my mom's feet and then Morris would act like he caught the mouse and take credit for its capture. We all laughed at how Morris stole Charlie's accomplishments. They were quite the pair. Charlie was mine and Morris claimed Kathy. He would follow her everywhere. The funniest thing that happened with Charlie and Morris though, was when we left them at the apartment one day while we went to my therapy. We had corn on the cob the night before and had thrown several pieces in the trash can in our kitchen. When we came home we found their litter box full of corn crap from them having eaten the left over pieces. We had to take Charlie and Morris to the farm at Vici when we later moved from the garage apartment to the Hi-Lo Apartments closer to the NWOSU campus. I'm not sure what fate Charlie met, but Morris stole a ride with dad to town under the hood of the car and dad said he ran off when he got to town.

Duke had told my dad that there was a good chance that we had a Product's Liability case and that there might be more in the way of a settlement from the manufacturer of the front end loader and the tractor. Duke filed a lawsuit against GB Front End Loaders and John Deere Company in the amount of 1.25 million dollars. Duke contended that the GB Front End loaders was at fault for not having a self-leveling device or fail safe switch on their front end loaders to prevent the bale from falling back onto the operator. He said that John Deere should be held liable for not having a rolling object or falling object device installed on the tractor to protect the operator from falling objects or from the tractor rolling over. To this day, I do not recall if the front end loader malfunctioned by continuing to raise the hay bale because the hydraulics stuck or if I actually had my hands on the raising lever of the loader itself. I guess I will never know the answer to that question.

CHAPTER 18

Time to Get Married

Duke advised Kathy and me that it would look better if we were married when our lawsuit went to trial. We were still planning to get married on December 12, 1979 but after Duke's advice we decided to get married earlier. Kathy's mom and dad did not approve of her staying with me after the accident and I couldn't blame them, if she had been my daughter I would have felt the same way. We didn't tell anyone that we were getting married early, instead we went to the court house in Alva and filed for a marriage license, got our blood tests done and found two witnesses to take with us to Vici to get married. Kathy's best friend at the time was Katie Huffman from Arnett who was going to college at Alva, and I chose Jim Peck to be my best man or the other witness. They rode with us in our new T-Bird to Vici and along the way we even got pulled over for Kathy speeding. He gave her a warning and we proceeded on our way.

I had contacted the Vici Church of Nazarene pastor Glendale Raines to see if he would agree to marry us before driving down there. He agreed and met us at the church, I had attended all of my life before falling out of God's grace. It was just Kathy and I, our two witnesses Katie and Jim and the pastor and his wife at the ceremony. His wife played the matrimony song on the organ and we said our vows, exchanged rings and I kissed the bride. Not the wedding Kathy had planned for but we were now legally married on October 4, 1979. Pastor Raines signed the marriage license and told us to have it filed back in Woods County where it was issued.

We decided to drive to the farm and tell my parents the good news. When we got there, no one was home. We thought it was odd so we got in touch with my brother Charles who told us that daddy had ran over himself the day before with his pickup and was in the Woodward Hospital. Evidently daddy had parked his pickup on an incline and gotten out to open a gate. He had not set the emergency brake and the pickup started rolling backwards. He tried to jump in the pickup but the door knocked him down and the front tire of the pickup rolled over his groin and hip. Mom had a bad gall bladder attack the same day and was also in the hospital. She had gotten upset when Buddy, the dog she was keeping for Willneta, had been run over.

We drove to Woodward to see mom and dad in the hospital and found out my sister Belinda was there about to deliver her second child Mikey, who was born the following day, October 5, 1979. We found mom on the second floor and dad and Belinda on the 3rd floor. Everyone was happy to hear our news. We said our good byes and took Katie and Jim back to Alva and spent our honey moon in our garage apartment. I knew that I had failed to give Kathy the wedding she had always planned on and I felt bad about it. In the later years I would pay for that when our own daughters got married.

We lived in that garage apartment from July 1979 to December 1979 and had lots of friends from college come over and played video games or poker with me. One night we had a big poker party and there were empty beer cans all over the apartment. Kathy had gone to her classes the next day and I was alone in bed. I heard a knock at the door. I yelled out "Come in". It was Kathy's dad, Dean Wolf. Kathy had finally told her parents that we were married. He decided to drop in and surprise us. Boy did he surprise us. I was never so embarrassed in my life. I decided that I had to straighten my act up and quit feeling sorry for myself. I can just imagine what Dean thought when he saw all of those empty beer cans. His father was an alcoholic and Dean had nothing to do with drinking. Now he had a paralyzed son-in-law married to his only child. What a disappointment I must have been to him. After that Dean and Della said that Kathy was on her own and that they would not be helping her with her college and living expenses and they doubted that she would follow through and even complete college. They knew that she would be permanently a hostage taking care of me. I felt like half of a man at this point in my life.

We moved to the Hi-Lo Apartments across from the girl's dormitory near the campus in January 1980 and lived there until we moved back to Woodward in May 1980. While living in these apartments, we had to get rid of our cats. Kathy lost her first set of wedding rings that I had bought her doing dishes one night. We never did find them so we bought another wedding set at Service Merchandise in Oklahoma City. Seems like that set cost around $600. Sometime in there we traded off my 1973 Cheyenne pickup and bought a 1978 Chevy pickup that had a diesel motor in it. I had hand controls installed in it and learned to how to drive with them. The thing I remembered most about that pickup was that you had to check the gasoline and add the oil. It burned a quart of oil every 250 to 300 miles.

Kathy and I after getting married in October 1979

CHAPTER 19

Back to College and the Lawsuit

The lawsuit that Duke filed in District court was moving along and we talked about me going back to college. We checked to see if I could enroll again at NWOSU in Alva but most of the freshmen classes were held in the Jesse Dunn building that had stairs going into the building. The building had four floors and no elevators, so it was totally inaccessible to me. We checked other colleges in Oklahoma and decided on Central State University in Edmond, Oklahoma.

We decided to move to Woodward, Oklahoma in May 1980 after Kathy had completed her spring semester and find jobs until we could move to Edmond to start college. Duke had offered me a job working as a paralegal at his law firm

Hieronymus, Hogden, Halley and Meyer that summer. Kathy found a job selling ads for a local newspaper, The Pennyshaver. We rented a two bedroom apartment on Kansas Street where we lived from May 1980 to August 1980.

While we lived at Woodward, my friend Matt Ray got a divorce and we agreed to let Matt live with us during the summer. Kathy, Matt and I refinished an old 1959 Starcraft boat that Matt owned. We put in a new floor and bought a new 1978 Johnson 55HP outboard motor on it. That summer we went out on Fort Supply Lake and Matt taught Kathy how to water ski. We hauled that boat to Kimberling City, Missouri on our vacation, where we broke down 3 miles from our dock and had to troll all of the way back. We found a 6 foot spoonbill catfish floating on the lake and pulled it up on the hull of the boat and took a picture then threw it back in the lake. We later found out that this was a great fish to eat. It had just been freshly hit by another boat when we found it in the lake. We had a lot of fun that summer with Matt but the summer came to an end and we had to think about going to college in August.

I liked working at the law firm and was even able to work on my own product's liability lawsuit that summer setting up depositions and such. I thought about maybe pursuing a degree in law but I was more of numbers person and therefore did not pursue that route. Now my original intention was to become an Industrial Arts Instructor and that is why I had chosen

NWOSU at Alva, but now my circumstances had changed so I had to change my career path. I decided to try accounting instead since I liked working with numbers. I enrolled at Central State University in the fall of 1980 with the help of Voc-Rehab, a state agency that helps handicapped people with pursuing jobs, but first we had to find a place to live in Edmond.

While living in Woodward we looked at mobile homes as an option for living. One of my brother's best friends owned a Lancer Mobile Home dealership in Woodward. His name was Steve Neagle and he helped Kathy and I pick out a floorplan that would accommodate my wheelchair and we ordered it, paying $30,000. We had all of the doors changed to 3 foot doors and widened the hallway. We were supposed to have the 1980 14'x 80 Lancer Mobile home delivered to Edmond just in time for us to start to college in August of 1980, but production fell behind and it was not completed when we started back to college. Instead, we had to rent a motel room for 2 weeks while waiting for our home. We were still living in the Red Carpet Motel off of Broadway and 15th Street in Edmond when we started to college.

Finding a lot to rent was our next hurdle. We had met a man who was building a new mobile home park north of Waterloo Road and Coltrane, but when we got to Edmond, he had not even started building the park. We looked in Edmond near the college but all of the lots were rented as well as a trailer park east of the college off of 2nd Street. We had a new 80' mobile home coming to Edmond and no place to park it. We remembered seeing a mobile home park back on Coltrane and Waterloo Rd. when we went to see the man about the new mobile home park. This one set back south of Waterloo Rd. and on the east side of Coltrane. The ladies' name was Lola Payne and the mobile home park she ran was run down and pretty disgusting but she had a vacancy right next to a big cottonwood tree which would provide some pretty good shade. I can't remember the exact amount we had to pay for lot rent but I think it was around $50 to $75 per month, which was pretty affordable for us at the time. We negotiated a lease with Lola and got the lot we wanted. It was here at Lola Payne's mobile home park that we met our lifelong friends Doug and Teri Barnes. They were from Tulsa, Oklahoma and were a year older than Kathy and I and had been married a year before us in 1978. Doug could make friends with anyone while Teri was shy, but she and Kathy became good friends, as did Doug and I. Doug was studying to be an Art major while Teri was studying to become a Registered Nurse. They never had any children at the time, just a large Irish Setter named Diamond. Their mobile home was a 12x65 which was just south of us near a big Mimosa tree.

Kathy had completed two years of college at Alva and was half way through her degree when we moved to Edmond. We figured that she would graduate in May of 1982. She had never really declared a major at Alva, but when she enrolled at Central State University she decided to major in Marketing and minor in Fashion Merchandising. Kathy had worked at a shoe store in Woodward from the time she was 12 years old and she loved going to Market in Dallas with the owners of F&W Shoes, Tom and Lois McDonald. She later worked at Wal-Mart when it opened in Woodward in 1977, and she loved working with the public. She found the job working at the Pennyshaver to be challenging work and realized that she had good marketing skills. I think these work experiences are what helped her make up her mind of what to pursue. But to be honest she was just trying to prove to her mom and dad that she could finish college and give them a diploma to prove it.

I decided to pursue a General Business and Accounting certificate program rather than pursuing a BS in Accounting. The certificate program would require me to take 15 hours of accounting plus other courses needed in a business setting. It was a 40 hour program and I should be able to complete it easily by the time Kathy completed her 4 year degree in Marketing and Fashion Merchandising. Turns out I ended up taking 21 hours of accounting, only nine hours short of what an Accounting degree required. Most of the classes I took were upper level classes and the basic classes taken as a Freshmen or Sophomore, I had not taken when I received my certificate.

I ended up with a total of 55 hours of credit, 15 hours more than required. One of the classes I had to take for the certificate program was Intermediate Typewriting. I had not taken Typewriting in high school mainly so I could avoid having Kate Moore as my instructor. Mrs. Moore had the reputation of straightening out unruly young men, and I felt like I fell into that class. Now I was regretting my decision in high school and having to learn something that had come so easy to my older brother Larry and sisters Belinda and Willneta. Because I did not know how to type, I had to take Beginning Typewriting before I could take Intermediate Typewriting. There was just one problem though about taking Typewriting at Central State University in Edmond, the classes were on the second floor of the Business Building and there were no elevators. Voc-Rehab and the college itself hired 5 young college students to carry me and my chair up and down the flight of stairs five days a week. They hired five instead of four young men just to be on the safe side so if one of the boys was sick, there would be a backup on hand. By the second semester, the college renovated the first floor with a typewriting room and I was able to take Intermediate Typewriting on the first floor without any assistance.

The Dean of the School of Business at CSU, Dr. James Perry was a very nice man and wanted to see me succeed at CSU. I still look back at my success at CSU and accredit a large part on his willingness to help me overcome physical barriers on the college campus. The ADA act would not be passed until in the 1990's so what he was doing for me at CSU was before it's time.

It had been 7 years since I had taken Algebra I in high school and I now had to take College Algebra as one of the courses for my accounting certificate program. The instructor passed out a quiz the first day with 25 problems to solve to gage our skills. I think I got 4 out of 25 of the problems correct. The next day the instructor gave us back the graded quiz and she asked me to stay after class. I explained that it had been over 7 years since I had taken Algebra I in my freshmen year of high school and had not taken Algebra II or Calculus. She advised me that I might want to take Intermediate Algebra and then take College Algebra the next semester. I told her that I would drop the class if I was not passing the class by mid-term. By mid-term I was making a 98% average in the class and went on to take Business Statistics where I also made a 98% average in the class. The classes I had the hardest time getting a good grade were Beginning and Intermediate Typewriting. I made a B in Beginning Typewriting and a C in Intermediate Typewriting. I just got too nervous during the timed typing tests and would only type like 55 words a minute with many mistakes. My brother Larry had taken Kate Moore in high school and could type 95 WPM with no mistakes on an old Underwood manual typewriter. I was using a new IBM Selectric typewriter in college but the difference was the typist not the typewriter.

In the fall of 1980 my lawsuit was moving along and was set to go to trial in November 1980. As you might remember, we sued for $1.25 Million. During the summer we made a film called "A Day in the Life of Jim Young", which showed all of the hardships I had to endure from living a life in a wheelchair. We went to trial in November and presented our portion of the case to the judge and jury. The film was shown like on the third day of trial and then we rested our case. It was now time for the judge to decide if we had cause and whether to dismiss John Deere and G.B. Frontend Loaders or dismiss one and keep the other. Duke, my attorney felt like our presentation had gone well but warned Kathy and I and my parents that the judge may very likely dismiss John Deere, saying that our case against them was not as strong as what it was against G.B. Frontend Loaders. During the recess between us presenting our case and the defendants presenting their case, both John Deere and G.B. Frontend Loaders made settlement offers to us. John Deere offered $75,000 to settle out of court and G.B. Frontend Loaders offered $325,000 to settle. We decided to accept both offers and the lawsuit was over. Of course, since we had gone all the way to court, my attorney got the 1/3 of settlement as his fees or $133,333.33, leaving Kathy and I with $266,666.67. We left a lot on the table from what we had originally sued for but we were able to leave court victorious and more importantly we were able to obtain college degrees for both of us. I think the first thing we bought with the money was a 1980 Chevy Blazer which was a white and maroon two tone with two doors. The rest of the money I invested in $100,000 worth of Municipal Bonds, $100,000 of Certificate of deposits. We were in a recession during this time and inflation had caused interest rates as high as 16% being paid on CDs. The two tax-free Municipal bonds that I invested in paid 12.25% on $50,000 and 10.4% on the other $50,000.

CHAPTER 20

1981: A Year of Highs and Lows

We began our second semester at Central State University in January 1981. I was finding that accounting was my correct chosen field of study and Kathy was loving Marketing. She even had some Marketing classes taught by Vince Orza, a local television news anchor on Channel 5 ABC in Oklahoma City. He would go on to run for Governor of Oklahoma a few years later. I was taking classes like Principles of Accounting, Business Law and Intermediate Typewriting, and Income Tax I. Our friendship with the Barnes next door grew more and more since we moved to Edmond. Doug was refurbishing a 1974 Vega station wagon that was painted green. He used to come over to our mobile home and play chess with me and we would watch our two favorite shows on television, MASH and the Benny Hill show. Doug painted water color paintings of Native Americans. He was quite good.

Kathy and I had bought two AKC registered Pekingese pups, a male and a female. We named the male Bandit and the female Bridget. We also found a white female kitten that we named Sophie. These animals were our kids at this stage of our lives, then one day probably in February, Kathy informed me that she had missed her period. She thought she might be pregnant. Could this be true? Had the doctor been wrong about us not being able to have children? Sure enough, Kathy did a pregnancy test and found an OBGYN named Betty Ayres in Edmond, who confirmed that she was pregnant and due in the middle of October. We did not have health insurance so we had to pay full price for our first child. We were so excited that God was blessing us with our own child. We told both of our parents and they too were shocked about the news. My dad pulled me aside one day when we went to visit them on the farm and asked me if I knew for sure that the baby was mine. I told him, "Yes I am certain it is". I have always wondered why he doubted the legitimacy of our first child but after finding out the true story of him being Barbara and Billy's real father, I kind of understand where he was coming from back then. My mom was of course overjoyed at hearing the news and I really don't know how Dean and Della felt about the news, but somehow, I figure they were a little apprehensive at first and wondered how I would be able to help take care of the child. We did not have any tests done to determine the sex of our child but instead we waited until birth to find out.

We both finished our spring semester at CSU and both of us decided to take summer classes so that we could get as many hours completed before our child came in October. Mom and dad had decided to retire from the farm and move into town. They had found a new 3-Bedroom brick home with 2 baths and a two car garage in the Cleveland Addition of Vici. It was the dream home Mom had always wanted. I advanced my parents the $64,500 so that they could buy the house in town and would collect it back when the farm sold. Daddy had just leased the farm land to Jerry Brace earlier in the year so we would have to wait until the lease expired before he could actually sell the farm. I was happy to be able to help them get the house and see them retire for once. They both had worked hard all of their lives and deserved a retirement in a new home with no worries. It was the weekend after my 21st birthday and Kathy and I had gone to Vici. We had gone to the liquor store and grocery stores to get boxes to help mom and dad pack up dishes and household goods and dropped them off at the farm.

We went back to Edmond to start our summer semester on June 8, 1981. I was in my Advanced Tax class in the Business Building on June 9, 1981 when Kathy opened the door and told me to come out into the hall. She told me that my dad had committed suicide between the house and barn on the farm and that my mom had found him. I would later find out that he had used my 12 gauge shotgun to shoot himself in the head. We got in the Blazer and I drove like a bat out of hell to get home. We probably made the 2 hour drive in less than 1-1/2 hours.

That first night we moved mama to her new house in town and all of us kids met out at the farm house and reminisced about old times and living on the farm. We buried daddy on June 11, 1981 which was Bill and Belinda's wedding anniversary. I just remember staring at that bronze closed casket setting in front of me at the Vici Church of the Nazarene. We were all devastated that he had committed suicide but in a way we all understood his reasons why. After he had run over himself two years earlier, he had to have hip surgery to replace the hip joint. Dad was just too old for the muscles and tendons to heal properly to keep the joint replacement in place. He had the hip pop out of place three times after the surgery and three times he had to be taken to Enid to have it put back in place. The third time the doctor told him that he needed to be in nursing home for six weeks in a full body cast for the hip to heal properly. I'm pretty sure it was while daddy sat in that nursing home that he decided to buy mom the house in town and further plan his own demise. I guess Belinda and Bill had talked with daddy on June 6, 1981 when they found a note he had written. This same note was found in his overalls the day he committed suicide. It read as follows: "I know you won't forgive me, but just forget me & all I might have done or should have done." W.E Young.

We decided that we needed to go ahead and sell the farm earlier than daddy had planned to, so on September 5, 1981 we held a Public Auction and sold the remaining 320 acres of farm land that were left plus the home place. I had to break the lease with Jerry Brace and refund him the lease rental and fuel costs he had already incurred in farming the land. Fortunately, Jerry understood the circumstance and agreed to do so.

Leo Helmick was the auctioneer and we sold the surface rights only of the 320 acres and reserved the mineral rights in mom's name. The land sold for $500 per acre, giving mom about $160,000 of which she repaid me the $64,500 for the house money I had advanced her and she was left with close to $100,000 to invest in bonds and CDs.

1981 had been a year of joy upon finding out that we were going to have a child, only followed by a low when daddy committed suicide but now it was getting close to the arrival of our first born. I'll never forget Betty Ayres arriving at the hospital in her cowboy boots with horse crap on them. She was a woman who spoke her mind and didn't take any crap. Needless to say she cleaned up and was there in her scrubs without the cowboy boots on when she delivered Jason Eric Young, weighing in at 7 pounds 9 ounces. He was truly a gift from God and we felt so blessed. He arrived on October 14, 1981 and left us on a high note for the year 1981. Because we had no health insurance he cost like $450 for the doctor and I think the hospital bill was like $900. I'm pretty sure you can't buy a baby that cheap today.

I always felt like Jason was perhaps a reincarnation of my dad and that my dad somehow knew that there would be more Young boys to carry on the name after he was gone.

CHAPTER 21

Juggling College and a Newborn

Raising a newborn while still trying to go to college was a challenge for both Kathy and I, but we worked out a system. Kathy would graduate in the summer of 1982 pretty much on track despite all of the distractions of my accident and taking care of me, my father's death and now being a new mother. She was bound and determined to prove to her parents that she could graduate from college no matter what life threw at her. She just wanted to hand her dad that piece of paper saying that she was a college graduate. Kathy has never ceased to amaze me throughout the 40 plus years I have known her. Her strong German ancestry has at times made her difficult to reason with, but inside she has a heart of gold that cares for those she loves and she will not let anyone mess with them. Her maternal instincts were instantaneous when Jason was born. Deep down I think she wanted a little girl but given the circumstances of what Dr. Stein had said about us not being able to have children, she was elated just to be able to have children. I felt the same way and just thanked God for the gift of our first born child.

Kathy was a senior in college and some of the classes she needed to graduate were only offered during the daytime so we decided that I would go to school in the evenings while she went during the day. I would take care of Jason during the day while Kathy went to college and she would take care of him while I took evening classes.

Kathy would take Jason over to Guthrie and Liberty lakes north of us and go fishing sometimes while I was in class. Jason loved playing with our Pekingese dogs Bandit and Bridget out in the front yard where we made a small pen for them. My niece Teresa Braudrick came and stayed with us for about a week while we lived at the trailer park and went fishing with us. We went down one of the roads back to Guthrie Lake after a rain and got stuck. Kathy and Teresa had to push me out and I got mud all over them. We laughed about it all the way back to our home. Teresa was great with Jason and we enjoyed having her stay with us.

With part of our settlement money, we bought a little brown metal building that we put by the big cottonwood tree.

We also bought a heavy duty 20 HP Sears Craftsman Garden tractor and implements, including a roto tiller, angle blade, a red wagon, a disc, a one bottom mold board plow and a mower that attached to the back. If I couldn't work on a farm I was going to at least grow a garden on our trailer lot. The soil around Edmond was nothing like that from Vici. It was hard red clay soil not sandy like that from Vici. We still were able to grow corn, potatoes, tomatoes and green beans. I guess the saying that you can take the boy from the farm, but you can't take the farm out of the boy was true.

Spring passed and summer came and both Kathy and I completed our degree and certificates program. I had made the Dean's Honor roll and had a 3.75 GPA with 55 hours completed. The only "C" I made was for Intermediate Typewriting, everything else was either an "A" or a "B". I ended up with 21 hours of accounting. I had an offer to work for Melvin Johnston as soon as we could get moved to Fargo, Oklahoma. Kathy's mom and dad came to our graduation ceremony in early August 1982 and helped us pack up the mobile home for moving. Dean brought his wheat truck to load the metal building onto and most of the garden tractor implements. I had a trailer for hauling the garden tractor itself. We hired Clyde Thomas from Fargo to pull the mobile home to Fargo.

We said our good-byes to Doug and Teri Barnes and pulled out of Lola Payne's trailer park ready to begin our new lives in

Fargo, Oklahoma. The trip to Fargo should have been our first clue that we might be making a mistake. On the way there we had like 3 blowouts on the mobile home. It was August and over 100 degrees when we moved, but Clyde was an experienced hauler and made it safely to Fargo with the Lancer mobile home. Kathy, Jason and her mother I think rode in the Blazer, Dean drove the wheat truck with the building and implements, etc. on board and I drove my pickup pulling a trailer with the garden tractor onboard.

CHAPTER 22

My First Professional Job

Before we moved to Fargo, we had made several trips up there to look for a lot to move our mobile home. We finally settled on a corner lot that contained 3 lots. On the corner of 4th and Ash in Fargo, there was a two bedroom stucco house with an old dilapidated detached garage. Next to it were two empty lots where some mobile homes had been parked. We bought all three lots including the house for $21,500 and had my ex-cousin Dale Johnston come and blade the two empty lots until they were level. Dale had been married to my 1st cousin Darlene Bowman and was also the brother of Melvin Johnston, whom I was going to work for. Clyde parked and blocked the Lancer Mobile Home on the far north lot and then we hired my brother Charles to come build a two car garage, an office and a covered porch on the south side of the mobile home. Charles also poured a nice patio and long concrete ramp that went up to the covered porch and entry door of the home. He built another ramp on the north side with a sidewalk that connected to the driveway he built in front of the two car garage. I then had Charles refurbish the old one car garage on the south lot and make it into my work shop for storing my garden tractor and implements. He poured a driveway in front of the shop and sidewalks around it for me. We then had new chain link fence built all around lots 2 and 3 where the mobile home sat and a small chain link fence around the shop and about 50 feet east of it to make a garden. We put a gate in between the garden and front yard fence.

When we moved to Fargo, there was already a family living in the house on the corner in Lot 1. I went over to visit them and to see if they would be interested in continuing to rent the house from me. There was an old man and his wife living there plus their adult daughter and one grandchild. After looking at the house I decided that it needed to be renovated itself, so I hired Charles to remove the wall between two bedrooms and make it into a large one bedroom house. I remember the grease on the walls and ceiling in the kitchen being disgusting and the house wreaked with grease and nicotine smells. After all was said and done we had about $68,500 total in the entire place including our home. That fall I tilled up the entire yard with my garden tractor and planted perennial rye grass. We had the only yard that was green during the winter and that needed mowed during the winter. In the spring, I tilled up the rye grass and planted Bermuda seed. We had one of the nicest yards in Fargo at that time.

Across the street from our rent house, lived an older couple named Brownie and Eva Thomas. They were Clyde Thomas parents, the man who moved our mobile home for us. Brownie reminded me of my Grandpa McDonald because he smoked roll your own cigarettes. He wore bibbed overalls like my dad and his fingers were yellowish orange from smoking his cigarettes all the way down to the ashes. Brownie was a small engine repair man so when I had trouble with my garden tractor he would help me out. Eva you could tell had German ancestry in her and spoke with authority. They were great neighbors and when I wasn't working at Melvin's I spent a lot of time visiting them.

We had our mobile home skirted with Masonite before winter had set in but now it needed painted to match the rest of the mobile home which was a cream color. Melvin told me about an old gentleman named Thurman Thomas, who I believe was Brownie's brother. He never used a spray gun or a roller but instead used a 6" wide horse hair brush. He painted our entire mobile home, the skirting and the two car garage for us for some ridiculously low price. He was one of the best painters I have ever seen.

Kathy decided to take a job in Woodward working at a flower shop. Her boss was Mary Meyers and she ran the Apple Basket Flower shop off of Main Street. Kathy found a baby-sitter to watch Jason while she worked, which turned out to be a girl from Harmon, Oklahoma named Carolyn Reed. Her maiden name was Hunter but she married my 7th grade English teacher's son Barry Reed. They lived in a huge two story log cabin in Woodward and had twin girls but no boys, so Barry got to play with Jason and they became buddies. While staying with them, Jason learned how to go up and down stairs. Jason never did learn to crawl but instead went straight to walking when he was about 9 months old.

While living at Fargo, we used to go eat out with my oldest Sister Barbara and her husband Joe. One night we were eating at Linda's, a nice steak house on the west edge of Woodward. The table had a table cloth on it and all of our plates and glasses of water were on the table cloth. Jason came up to the table and grabbed the table cloth and gave it a big pull and jerked the table cloth off of the table without spilling anyone's water. We laughed in disbelief at what he had done. He was less than 2 years old at the time.

I started working for Melvin Johnston, CPA on August 15, 1982 making $7.00 per hour or $10.50 with overtime. Melvin had just filed the final extensions for the 1981 tax year that were now due on or before October 15, 1982. I loved my tax courses at CSU and had made A's in both Income Tax and Advanced Tax, but that was all book learning, I was now going to learn how it was really done. One of the courses I had to take was office machines, which include running a ten key adding machine. Melvin quickly showed me the meaning of footing and cross-footing 13 columnar pads which seemed to be the normal way of tax clients to track their business income and expenses. I became quite efficient running a ten key, much better than I was typing on a typewriter.

Melvin had hired my sister Belinda straight out of high school to work in his CPA firm in 1973 and now I was working for him. He had passed the CPA exam on the first sitting in like 1968 and had won honors for 2nd or 3rd highest score in the state at that time. By the time I had started to work for him, he had been doing people's tax returns or business financials for 14 years. He showed me a fail proof bank reconciliation form that I still use today to reconcile my checkbook. Melvin had several women working in the office when I started. There was Pam Rowe who was his main bookkeeper in the back, plus Jo Reineger who helped post entries to customer's financials and do payroll reports. One of Melvin's nieces, Dana Johnston worked for him during tax season, and John Latta would help him prepare tax returns during tax season. Around December of 1982, my sister Willneta and her husband Kerry moved back to Oklahoma and she started working for Melvin. They lived in their 5th wheel RV just north of us.

Melvin had told me that I could work as many hours as I wished to and that he would pay me the $10.50 an hour for anything over 40 hours, so I used to take work home with me and would go out to my office after supper and work until bedtime or 10:00. I kind of got in a bad habit of working too much and became a workaholic. I was neglecting Kathy and Jason, plus prior to moving to Fargo, we learned that Kathy was pregnant again. I prepared somewhere between 350 to 400 tax returns while working for Melvin, plus I manually prepared Cash Flow statements for the businesses that we prepared computer generated Income Statements and Balance Sheets. The computer software we had did not generate a computer Cash Flow Statement.

Kathy had bought a little mauve flower dress with ruffles around the sleeves when she found out she was expecting our second child. She now had that little dress hanging on the door knob of the front bedroom door anticipating that she would be able to use it on child number two. Once again, we did not know what we were going to have and she just knew the second baby would be a girl. Having moved from Edmond to Fargo, Kathy had to find a doctor in Woodward to deliver our second child. We chose Leo Meese, MD to be her doctor. I think he charged $600 for a delivery, up $150 from when Jason was born. This baby would be born at Woodward, Oklahoma in the same hospital I was born in 1960.

I remember a snow storm coming on March 19, 1983 when it came time to take Kathy to the hospital in Woodward. We actually took Lamaze classes in Woodward to prepare for this birth. The first birth was pretty rough for Kathy and for me. We hoped the breathing classes would help make this birth easier for both of us. I'll never forget what was playing on television the night we went to the hospital for the delivery, "Leave It to Beaver", the 25th anniversary show. Well, Kathy was disappointed not being able to use that little flower dress as our second son was born that evening. Cody Derek Young weighed 8 pounds 4-1/2 ounces. Jason now had a little brother to play with. Our little family was growing. God had again blessed us with yet another gift and we rejoiced.

I got through my first tax season or April 15 deadline that year and was gaining more and more confidence in my accounting capabilities. I knew this was the profession God wanted me. My lawyer had tried to talk Kathy and I into opening a liquor store after we got our settlement, but somehow that didn't seem like the thing to do after having been a teenage alcoholic.

I planted a big garden out by the shop and raised corn, potatoes, green beans, watermelons, and cantaloupes that summer. I also planted several Concord grape vines along the west chain-link fence. We decided to take a trip to Branson with the boys in June or July so we left our dogs Bandit and Bridget at the house and asked Willneta and Kerry to watch them. When we came back from Branson, we could not find Bandit. We later found out that he had been shot by the local town cop, Steve Wade for chasing chickens. He and Bridget had dug out of our chain-link fence and had been chasing an old couple's chickens several blocks away. The cop was a little gung ho and decided to execute rather than capture the male dog, Bandit. He unloaded his .357 revolver on Bandit hitting him at least three times. We made the cop take us out to where he had buried our dog and dig him up. Needless to say, we were not happy and we let the town board know it. When Melvin took the town's side on the matter, we decided maybe staying in Fargo was not to be. I gave Melvin my resignations but promised to stay until the last tax deadline, October 15, 1983. Meanwhile, we made some trips back to Edmond and looked for a house to purchase and I decided to go back to college and get my BS in Accounting. Kathy never was really happy living in Fargo after having all of the conveniences of living in and around Oklahoma City.

CHAPTER 23

Back to Edmond and the CPA Exam

We went to Edmond one weekend and drove through an addition, on the west side of town that had several houses for sale. The first house was a four bedroom house but only 1,200 square feet. The halls were too narrow and bathroom doors too small, plus all of the bedrooms were small. The realtor then took us to a house on the other end of the street. It too was a four bedroom house but this time it was around 2,100 square feet with a large living room and master bedroom. The halls were wider and the floorplan was perfect for us. It had an above ground pool with a bubble top in the backyard. We fell in love with it and signed the contract on it that day. They were asking $115,000 and we were young and eager to find a home and did not even think about offering them less. We ended up paying down $60,000 and financing the remaining $55,000 over a 30 year mortgage. I think our house payments ended up being $514.28 per month with the escrow payments included.

When we got back to Fargo after that weekend I told Melvin that I was going back to college to finish my accounting degree and as I promised I completed my employment with him until October 15, 1983, a total of 14 months from start to finish. I think Melvin was surprised that I would leave Fargo after spending so much time and money on our place, but looking back it was the best thing I could have done for me and my family. Who would have thought losing a dog could have changed the path our lives took, but it did.

Kathy had a miscarriage a couple months after giving birth to Cody. She would later find out that she was pregnant with our third child, who was now due in July, 1984.

I enrolled again at Central State University the spring semester of 1984, this time to finish my accounting degree. Because I had taken mainly upper level courses during my first couple years at CSU, I now needed to take my basic classes normally taken during your freshmen and sophomore years. When I went to college straight out of high school in 1978, I never had the desire to do well. When I went back in 1980 my mental disposition had changed and I went back to make something out of myself. This time I had a clear vision of graduating with an accounting degree and trying to take the CPA exam.

We moved to our new address 1204 South Taurus in October 1983. Our neighbors across the street were a nice Catholic family. The parent's names were Joe and Mary Jo Fischer and at that time they had five children but were expecting their sixth child. Joe worked at Safeway in Edmond which would later become a Homeland Grocery store. They were a great family to live across from and our kids and their kids became best of friends.

While I was going back to college, I decided to go ahead and prepare tax returns on the side to make extra money during tax season. I never had that many clients at first so things were pretty tough. We had our investment income in the way of CD Interest and Municipal Bond interest which helped make the house payment and utilities. Kathy decided to go to work while I went back to college. She found a job doing wedding dress alterations at a place called JJ Kelly's in Oklahoma City. Her talent never ceased to amaze me. She had done floral arrangements at Woodward while we lived at Fargo, now she was completely taking apart thousands of dollar wedding dresses and putting them back to together and adding sequins or whatever to make them even more pretty. I think this was also around the time that she started to do tuxedo rentals for the grooms and his groomsmen, not to mention making show choir dresses for young ladies in high school. Was there any-thing that she could not do?

I made it through my first semester back in college and I think I was in summer school when our third child arrived. Kathy was finally able to use that mauve floral dress as Ashley Marie Young arrived on the scene weighing in at 8 pounds 13 ounces. We still did not have health insurance so I think Ashley costs like $900 to the doctor and over $1,000 for the hospital stay. Dr. Tim Syler was supposed to be Kathy's doctor, but the night she went into labor he was not on call so Dr. Daniel Woi-wode delivered her instead. While cutting the umbilical cord Ashley kicked her leg up and he accidentally cut her little leg making a "V" mark on her leg. Ashley got her first two stitches on her birthdate. Kathy's friend from college, Katie Huffman had come over to our house to watch the boys while Kathy and I had gone to the hospital. Dean and Della would arrive shortly thereafter to help after Ashley was born.

Joe, our neighbor had a little fishing boat and we took it Guthrie Lake where he, Kathy, Jason and I went fishing. We had bought Jason a new Snoopy fishing rod and this was his first fishing lesson. He leaned back to throw his line in and instead released the entire rod throwing it into the lake and it sank to the bottom. We laughed as we watched it sink. Another time we went to Guthrie Lake with the two boys and had come back to the house. All of my tackle boxes and fishing poles were still in the back of my 1982 GMC we bought while living in Fargo. In the tackle box I had a fish filet knife that was razor sharp. I was across the street talking with Joe Fischer when I looked over and saw Cody with the filet knife. I hollered over at him and Jason and told them that they better put that knife back in the tackle box where it belonged. I continued talking to Joe when Jason came across the street and told me that Cody couldn't get the knife out of the truck. I told him that he better get it put up. A little bit later Jason came back and said the pickup was going down. I said "What do you mean going down?" I went over to see what he was talking about. Cody had stuck the knife into the sidewall of one of my back tires on the pickup and had pulled it out releasing all of the air out of the tire. He then tried to mend the tire by putting some first aid spray on the hole and putting two band aids across it. It was hard to get mad at him even though he had ruined an almost new tire, but the first aid treatment made us all laugh at his ingenuity of trying to fix the tire.

I completed college in May of 1986 with a total of 33 hours of accounting courses and was concerned about finding a job after graduating. I had gone to the placement office at the college to see what I needed to do. They told me that most companies interviewed students in the fall and that I had missed that crucial interview process.

On May 8, 1986 I was out in our garage sweeping the floor when one of our neighbors who lived behind us yelled at me.

He said you better get those kids in the house because there is a tornado coming. Sure enough I looked around the house and you could see the tornado lifting up particles into the sky coming off of the housing addition just one mile west of where we lived. It had hit the Fairfield addition on 15th and Santa Fe. We got the kids into the middle bathroom and hunkered down under the bathroom sink that had an opening. College graduation for me was the next day and we were trying to clean and get the house presentable for Dean and Della who were coming to watch me graduate. Kathy and the kids ended up going over to the Fairfield Addition that next day and helped pick up debris caused from the tornado. Dean and Della arrived and we went to Wantland Stadium for my graduation.

I figured I would be one of the last students called to receive my diploma because of my last name being Young and at the end of the alphabet, but they called students graduating with honors first. I hadn't realized that I was even graduating with honors, but I graduated Magna Cum Laude with a 3.8 GPA and received my diploma as one of the first recipients. I think that was the first time I had seen Dean and Della proud of me, which meant a lot to me.

As I mentioned, the placement office never gave me much of a chance of finding employment since I had missed the fall interviewing process and had pretty much told me to come back in the fall and try again. I did get a couple of interviews though in the spring interviewing process. Because of my high GPA, I had a couple of the Big Eight Accounting firms interview me. Deloit Touche and Arthur Andersen were the two I remember having interviews with and then there was a local accounting firm called Criswell, Hall and McIntosh that I interviewed with. There were 16 candidates that interviewed for one position at the local accounting firm. I made the cut all the way down to two candidates for the job opening. In the end the other candidate got the job. Later, Don Criswell the Managing Partner of the firm told me that he was leaning towards me but he was afraid that I would remind him of his wife too much. You see his wife was from Vici and they had just gotten married and were traveling back to Arkansas I think, when a tractor running a brush hog along the highway through an object through their car window and killed her. He never had really recovered from losing her so tragically and he was afraid that I would remind him of losing her. She was the daughter of Keith Jones who worked for the town of Vici Water Department. Keith Jones and my mom had actually been in the same class in high school even though my mother never did graduate. Mom told me the tragic story after I told her about my interview with Don Criswell.

Since I was not able to get a job in May 1986 I decided that I needed to study for the CPA exam, so I enrolled in the Becker CPA Review course being held at the Bishop McGuinness High School in June 1986. Before I started the review course I decided to build our kids a log cabin in the back yard out of landscape timbers. The log cabin became a neighborhood project and I had several neighbors including Joe Fischer, Frank Wride and some other Safeway employees they knew helping me build the cabin. I built the floor of the cabin on our back patio and had them move it under the cottonwood tree to where it would go. I then went as high as I could go with the landscape timbers and they helped me go the rest of the way up to about 6'. Then I laid out the design for the trusts for the roof and built the individual trusts on the patio and had the neighbors install them for me. Another neighbor who lived behind us did the planking of the roof and the shake shingles. I used a chainsaw to cut out the windows and door and framed the windows and doorway and built a door out of pine wood boards. I then built a set of kitchen cabinets for the inside and a lean to porch. We completed the log cabin just in time for my Becker CPA Review Course to start on my birthdate of June 4, 1986. It was truly a neighborhood effort and most of the wives of the men who helped were jealous that I could get their husbands to help me when they couldn't get them to do anything. I just told the wives that all they had to do was give them a beer to get them to work. That log cabin resided in the back yard even after we sold the house in 1996 and I don't think they tore it down until about 2016.

I took the Becker CPA Review Course all summer which costs me like $900 to take. I sat for the CPA exam at the Oklahoma City Myriad Convention Center in November 1986. It was 3 days or 19 hours of pure torture. When I got through taking the tests I don't think I could even tell you my name. I was mentally drained. I had studied solid for two months prior to taking the exam and in fact Kathy took the kids and moved over to stay with Katie Huffman the week before the exam to give me peace and quiet to study. Later that month the fall interviews were held at Central State University and again I interviewed with some Big Eight Accounting firms but this time I interviewed with a large Oil and Gas conglomerate company, Kerr-McGee Corporation. I interviewed with a man named Mike Rauh, who was the Controller of the Corporation and was from Alva, Oklahoma. We hit it off instantly because of our similar childhoods of being raised on a farm and him being from Alva where I had started to college. I was invited to a second interview to be held at Kerr-McGee's headquarters downtown Oklahoma City. I was nervous when I interviewed with the corporate CFO John Linehan, but after talking with him I found out that he too had come from a farm background and he appreciated someone with a strong work ethic. I think it was about a week when I heard back from Kerr-McGee and they extended me an offer to work provided I could pass the mandatory drug test. I started my employment with Kerr-Mc-Gee on December 9, 1986. About a month later I received the results from my CPA exam which showed that I passed all four parts the first time. I became a CPA in January 1987.

CHAPTER 24

Wesley Medical Reunion

T he year of 1987 started off well for me. I had just started to work at Kerr-McGee Corporation as an Accounting Management trainee, making a salary of $23,000 per year. As such I would get the opportunity to rotate to different subsidiaries and jobs within the conglomerate. Not only that but I had gotten back my CPA Exam results and I was now a new CPA. A month later we found out that Kathy was pregnant with our fourth child, who was to be born in November 1987.

I loved my job at Kerr-McGee and felt like I had a lot to offer them in the experience I had gained from working for Melvin Johnston, as well as they had a lot to teach me by rotating me through the different departments. My first boss was Eldon Rogers in Corporate Accounting. He was probably the best manager I had while working for KM. I worked there until May 1987 when I was rotated to General Accounting in the Exploration and Production division. From there I rotated to Revenue Accounting and then International accounting. I would go on to work my way up from a Grade 10 management trainee to a Grade 18 Senior Business Analyst in Information Technology department when I would leave KM after over 20 years of service in 2007. After KM I worked for Noble Energy, in Ardmore, Oklahoma for another 8 years, retiring in 2015.

It was the summer of 1987 when I received a letter informing me about a reunion to be held in Wichita, Kansas for the Wesley Medical Center rehab unit. It had been 8 years since I had been back to the rehab unit. It would be interesting to see some of the old gang that I had spent time with in the rehab unit. Even ole Dr. Stein with the bad bedside manner was supposed to be there. Kathy and I and our three kids loaded up in the 1984 Chevy Suburban and headed for Wichita.

They held the reunion at an outdoor park in Wichita away from the hospital itself. My old friend Marty Hochman along with his brother Myron and his wife and child were there. Frank Evans from Braman, Oklahoma was there with his mother. Bob Holgerson and his new wife were there. I can't remember if Kris Jackson was there or not but I know Jim Main wasn't because he died about 6 months after I got out of the hospital with Legionaire's disease. I do think his wife Joanne came to the reunion. There were several of the nurses from our floor that came and both of the physical therapists were there. And then I saw him, Dr. Paul S. Stein. He was sitting at one of the covered picnic tables drinking an iced tea.

I rolled up next to Dr. Stein and said, "Do you remember me?" He turned around and faced me and said "Yes, I do." I said, "I know you remember, Kathy who was my fiancé at the time, but I want to introduce you to my son, Jason and my second son Cody and my daughter Ashley, our fourth child is due in November." I said, "You told me that I would never be able to walk again, or have children." To which he replied, "Well we are not right all of the time, and congratulations to you on your family."

On November 29, 1987 we had our fourth child, a little girl we named Chelsea Tanae Young, who weighed 8 pounds 8 ounces. God had yet blessed us with our fourth gift. Chelsea was our free baby because for once we had maternity insurance that covered both the doctor and hospital costs. In between Ashley and Chelsea, Kathy had a second miscarriage which I know was hard on Kathy.

Ashley, Jason, Cody and Chelsea taken in 1990

CHAPTER 25

Religion in My Life

I was raised in the Church of the Nazarene in Vici, Oklahoma from the time I was little until I turned 15 and just stopped going to church. I knew there was a God and believed that Jesus Christ had been sacrificed and died on the cross to save all of us from our sins. I feared the wrath of God if I disobeyed him and learned at an early age not to lie for fear of retribution in some shape or form. My conscience would tell me when I had done something bad and make me feel horrible until I had prayed for God to forgive me, so I learned how to forgive others in the same manner.

My class had its fair share of students who went to the Nazarene church I attended. There was Carrie Badley, Connie Woods, Eddie Berry, Kenny Campbell and myself that went there. My sisters and I always attended vacation bible school during the summer and drank the grape Kool-Aid and ate the sugar and oatmeal cookies the mothers baked or brought for refreshments. We pledged allegiance to the American flag, pledged allegiance to the Bible and sang "Onward Christian Soldiers" each day. We made crafts with Janie Campbell like birdhouses and macaroni art during our craft hour and learned how to pray to Jesus while teachers like Mamie Cox, Ima Jean Helmick, or Jackie Jones read us Bible stories that we took to heart. We learned Bible scriptures each day that we repeated by memory at the closing ceremonies that next Sunday.

It wasn't until my teenage years or about 15, that I started rebelling against God and quit going to church. Little did I know at that time God would help me find my way back at age 25 after having our third child.

You may ask why we went to the Nazarene church and not the Church of the First Born that my Great Grandfather John McDonald had help found in the early 1900's or the Christian Church that my Grandpa Young attended faithfully during his later years. I guess the answer was because of my Aunt Mabel and her husband Carl Kruse and my Aunt Freeda and her husband Albert Bowman. I'm sure these two sisters had a great deal of influence over my dad just as Aunt Mabel would have over me when I was lost in my 20's.

Aunt Mabel and Uncle Carl Kruse were evangelists in the Nazarene church and went from town to town crusading and bringing people to Christ. They lived in Bethany, Oklahoma but travelled all over the United States as evangelists. The Nazarene religion is one of the younger denominations of religions in the United States but it is not much different than other denominations like the Methodist or Baptists. We still believe in the holy trinity of God, Jesus and the Holy Spirit.

When I was a teenager I strayed away from God and went down the wrong path. My conscience kept tugging at me that I needed to change my ways or I was going to regret my decisions. God has a way of helping one find his path back to salvation and repentance; little did I know what God had in store for me at such a young age of 18-1/2 years to get me back on the right path.

It was on drive up to Vici, Oklahoma in 1985 that I decided that to get back on the right path with God. I was taking my Aunt Mabel to the funeral of her sister and my Aunt Freeda Bowman. She said to me, "Jimmy you have three beautiful children and you really need to get those kids in a church so that they know God." I told her that my conscience had been eating on me for some time and I knew that I needed to get back to church myself. I was so busy talking with her that I failed to notice that I was speeding. About that time, I looked in my rear view mirror to see an Oklahoma Highway Patrol officer with his red lights on. I pulled over and he approached my pickup. My Aunt Mabel, intervened and said, "Officer, we were just visiting away and I guess my nephew must have not noticed that he was speeding. He is a good boy and I sure would appreciate it if you would just spare him a ticket this one time. We are on our way to my sister's funeral at Vici." The officer said, "I am just giving you a warning this time but please pay attention to the speed limit." He drove away and we proceeded on to Vici, but I did not forget our conversation and I started taking my family to the Edmond First Church of the Nazarene.

The pastor at the Edmond First Church of the Nazarene was Terry Rohlmeier in 1985. He was a great pastor and I remember him always calling for people to come to the altar and be forgiven of their sins. I would always stick up my hand to be prayed for but I could never muster up the nerve to go to the altar. We had a revival later that year and Pastor Terry invited evangelists Terry and Laquita Jones to come speak at our church. Terry Jones had been afflicted with ALS or the Lou Gehrig's disease. He was taking snake venom shots to treat the disease. His sermons inspired me to come down to the altar one of those nights at revival and I was a changed man after that. No more needing alcohol to cope with my problems. I gave my soul to God that day and I was saved and all of my sins were washed away. After that we began to tithe our income to the church and amazing things started happening for us. Over the years Kathy and I have been tested many times but together our faith has grown stronger and stronger. God has delivered us through good times and bad times but we have never turned away from God.

You might ask me if I was ever mad at God for allowing me to get hurt and ending up in a wheelchair the rest of my life. To that question, I say, "No". I never did blame God for what happened to me but instead I use myself as an example of what could happen if you do not follow the path God is leading you. I have stressed this over and over to my children throughout the years.

Kathy and I in 2012

CHAPTER 26

Summation and Final Thoughts

While writing this book I had mixed emotions remembering both good times and bad times. There were tears of joy and tears of sorrow. At the time of writing this book I have not lost any of my siblings, though all of us are growing older and I know it's just a matter of time before we start losing some. I briefly touched on the story about my mother and her struggle with cancer in 1992 and how all seven of us kids came together to show her the kind of love she deserved from us, for all of the love she showed us. I now have two siblings that are the age she was when she died or older and that scares me because I know some day I may have to go to their funerals or they to mine. Only God knows for sure.

I kind of made a deal with God when I got hurt that I would not have to suffer forever in this chair but that he would take me peacefully when it was my time. It has been over 40 years since my accident and I have seen a lot in my short 59 years on this earth, but I could not have done it without my sweet wife. Kathy has been my rock and my soulmate and we just celebrated our 40th wedding anniversary on October 4, 2019. If anyone deserves a place in Heaven, it is her. She could have abandoned me when I got hurt, but she didn't. Instead God blessed us with four beautiful children that we still love today despite what they might have done over the years, we will always show unconditional love for them. He then gave us 10 beautiful grandchildren that we love dearly. I am sorry that I did not include the births of each of the grandchildren in the book but I had to decide where to end this book and after the birth of the 4th child, it seemed like an appropriate place to end it.

Writing this book has been therapeutic to me. I realized that I had a lot of things hidden especially during my teenage years that I was not proud of. I know I was not a good son for all of the worries I put my parents through. I just hope I turned out to be a better father and grandfather to my children and grandchildren and that they will now understand who I was and what I became, because of my life experiences and going down the wrong path and how God got me back on the right path.

I would like to say a special thanks to my brothers Billy, Charles and Larry and my sisters Barbara, Belinda and Will-neta for helping me fill in the blanks of things I had forgotten. I love each and every one of you. And to my wife Kathy, I love you and thank you for always being there and for molding me into the man I became.

THE END

APPENDIX 1

Below is an obituary I found of Dr. Benson, the Union Army doctor who with his wife took in two orphaned boys named William Edward and Charles Henry Young. He allowed them to keep their last names of Young but gave them a home and raised them to adults. Charles Henry was my grandfather and who knows what might have happened to these boys had the generous doctor and his wife not taken them in.

Obituary of D.L. Benson

D. L. Benson

Born 1836 Died 1912 buried in the Hillcrest cemetery. He was a Union Doctor

MO online death certificate #41912; son of Samuel Benson and Polly?

Published December 5, 1912 in Mountain Grove Journal:

The little town of Dawson was sadly shocked by the sudden and unexpected death of Dr. D. L. Benson, which occurred about noon last Saturday in Mr. Smalley's store. The Doctor had just returned from a drive and took his team to the shop to get it shod. He then went to Mr. Smalley's and ordered his dinner, and while sitting down to wait for his meal to be prepared, he fell from his seat a lifeless corpse. The funeral service was held at Friendship church at twelve o'clock Sunday, conducted by C. C. Haggard, after which the remains were taken to Mountain Grove for burial.

Dr. D. L. Benson, of Mountain Grove, Wright Co., Missouri, was born in Perry County, Illinois, in 1836, and is the son of Samuel and Mary (Baker) Benson, and grandson of Daniel Benson, who was a native of Ireland, and who immigrated to America, locating in Tennessee, where he died. Samuel Benson was a native of

Bedford County, Tenn., born in 1806. When about eighteen years of age he immigrated to Boone County, Missouri, and remained there for about two years, when he went to St. Louis and worked at his trade, that of a stone mason. While in St. Louis he married Miss Baker, and soon afterward moved to Perry County, Illinois. where he followed agricultural pursuits the rest of his life. He died in March, 1888. Mary (Baker) Benson was born in Illinois in 1810, and died in 1886. They were the parents of thirteen children, three now living. Dr. D. L. Benson was the third child in order of birth. He grew to maturity on a farm in Illinois, and received his education in the common schools of his native county. Later he read medicine under a preceptor, but before practicing he married Miss Esther Staton, who was also born in Perry County, Illinois, in 1842, and reared within half a mile of her husband. Dr. Benson practiced medicine in Perry County, Illinois, and when forty years of age moved to Mountain Grove, Wright County, and his was the fifth family in the town. Here he continued the practice of his profession, and is next to the oldest practitioner in the place. He is strictly temperate in his habits, and has for many years been an elder in the Christian Church. Dr. Benson is an inveterate hunter, and every fall abandons his business and takes his annual hunt. During pioneer times he killed seventeen deer at one lick, from May until the 1st of August, and he has killed deer on what is now the public square of the town. He was surveyor of Perry County, Illinois, for fourteen years and is one of the successful practitioners of the town in which he now lives. Source: Goodspeed's 1889 History of Wright Co., Missouri.

DISCLAIMER

All of the events written in this book are nonfictional and reflect my best recollections of the events portrayed. In the event you as a reader of this book do not agree with my recollection of the events, I apologize and realize one person's memory may differ from another, but I wrote this book based on my individual recollection or memory. As such I meant no harm or ill will to anyone I mention in the book by name, for this is not my nature.

ABOUT the AUTHOR

Jim and Kathy Young – Sept 2015

Jim Young is a 59 year old retired CPA who has been confined to a wheelchair since he was 18-1/2 years old. He was raised by elderly parents on a wheat/dairy farm near Vici, Oklahoma and then attended his first year of college only to drop out after 10 weeks. His life changed dramatically after he found employment on a corporate farm where he sustained a broken back from a round hay bale accident. Were it not for the love and encouragement of his fiancé, Kathy, Jim may well have given up on life itself, but through her persistence they went on to get married, build a life together and raise four children, yielding them ten beautiful grandchildren. They just celebrated their 40th wedding anniversary and have grown together in their faith of God throughout the years.

Jim, a teenage alcoholic, would learn that God had a different plan for his life as he led Jim down a different path. Jim would eventually go back to college where he graduated with honors and passed the CPA exam the first sitting. He went on work for two independent Oil and Gas companies for over 28 years and retired in 2015 to enjoy his grandkids and spend more time with his wife, Kathy.